Through the Fire
Without Burning

by Dumitru Duduman

The True Story of a Romanian Pastor
Facing Communist Persecution

───────────────

"When thou passeth through the waters, I will be with thee; and through the rivers, they shall not overflow thee: when thou walkest through the fire, thou shall not be burned; neither shall the flame kindle upon thee. For I am the Lord thy God..."
— Isaiah 43:2&3a (KJV)

TABLE OF CONTENTS

PREFACE

This second edition of *Through The Fire Without Burning* has many changes from the first edition. Even the title has been restored to it's original form. These changes were necessary to correct errors that affected the accuracy - **but not the integrity** - of the original book. We feel a brief explanation is in order.

In 1986 Dumitru Duduman was approached by individuals who wanted to publish his experiences in a book. After much prayer, Brother Duduman agreed.

The book was dictated by Brother Duduman in Romanian, and translated to English for publishing. Then, it was turned over to others for help in editing and composition. The first edition was the result of a combined effort from many individuals. Those people helped in a way that words can not express. Our sincere thanks to those people is insufficient. May the Lord reward them for all their efforts.

Unfortunately, because several people were working simultaneously on the manuscript, various events were transposed, duplicated and eliminated. Unable to read English, Brother Duduman had no way of knowing the extent of some of the changes that were made to his original manuscript.

Since the finished work was a long time in coming, and being anxious to get the message out, it was sent directly to those wanting to see it published.

There were many roadblocks set by Satan in the efforts to get the book in print. It was only through the mostly volunteer efforts of his many friends that the first edition - *Through the Fire* - was finally ready for press.

Due to the many years of delays, and the final rush to get the book printed, it wasn't until Brother Dudduman had a published copy read to him that he discovered how many changes had been made to the original manuscript. But, because the changes didn't affect the overall **integrity** of the book, there was no need to reprint the first edition.

However, with this second edition, *Through the Fire Without Burning*, the errors have been corrected (including the title), and the original testimony written by Dumitru Duduman is more accurately reflected.

Now, read on and learn what it means to go *Through The Fire Without Burning*.

INTRODUCTION

Dumitru and his wife Maria are from Northern Romania and lived on a small farm close to the Soviet border. He pastored a small country church near their farm.

Over an 18 year period he delivered hundreds of thousands of Bibles and aids to the Soviet Union. In 1980 Dumitru delivered over 100,000 New Testaments which were used extensively at the Moscow Olympics.

In August of 1980 Dumitru was arrested, imprisoned and interrogated for five months. He was beaten almost every day and repeatedly shocked in an electric chair.

Arrest and interrogation became a continuous way of life for Dumitru. In 1983 he was hung by his waist and beaten on three different occasions. He suffered nine broken ribs and today has deformities on his rib cage.

Finally, the authorities gave Dumitru three choices; a mental hospital, prison... or expulsion to the United States.

The choice was hard for Dumitru because of his loyalty to his homeland, but he felt his first loyalty was to God.

They packed their clothes and most prized possessions, but the officials refused to let them take anything, so they left their homeland and friends empty-handed.

God had a reason for bringing Dumitru to this country and has given him a message for America. The message is hard and many people will be unable to receive it, but the Lord has promised a victory to those who will listen. That message is part of the amazing contents of this book.

Throughout Dumitru's life, God has clearly kept His hand on him. The Lord's protection has carried him through persecutions that should have left him dead. Without God's divine intervention, Dumitru would not be here today. He is a living example of God's promise of protection to those who will put their trust in the Lord. As the Bible promises, Dumitru Duduman has truely walked *Through the Fire Without Burning.* (Isaiah 43:2)

Through the Fire
Without Burning

by Dumitru Duduman

Chapter One

A CHILDHOOD PORTRAIT

From thousands of miles across the sea, memory carries me back to Romania – the land of my birth. In that beautiful, historic country I was born Dumitru Duduman on July 14, 1932. It is there that my heart still beats. Although exiled in 1984, the love of my homeland still surges through my veins, and the hope of helping those whom I left behind still quickens my pulse.

Romania, part of the Eastern Bloc, has about twenty million inhabitants. Bordered by Poland, Bulgaria, Yugoslavia, the USSR, and Hungary; Romania has seen centuries of war and turmoil. Since 1600, Romania's soldiers have been conquerors. In the past, her wise kings and rulers, understanding that God was the one who allowed their victories, constructed great cathedrals as monuments to their triumphs.

Those great churches are in the loveliest sections of Romania, and are filled with invaluable artifacts. They are at Putna, Voronet, Sucevita, and Neamtului. Many of these churches were built in the northern part of the country by Stephen the Great. Today, tourists visit them to see exquisite paintings, sculptures, golden statues and other fabulous works of art.

1

Since 1947, however, the country has been controlled by the Communists. The Russians do not build churches in honor of their military conquests. Instead, they destroy whatever places of worship they can find.

Oh, but Romania! Despite her seemingly endless struggles, she remains a breathtakingly lovely little corner of Europe. The country is crowned by spectacular high mountains. From their snowcapped peaks, forests roll across the foothills, and crystal-clear rivers flow through verdant farmlands. These rivers are rich in fish. The woods that grow along their banks are dappled with shadows and scattered with flower-filled little meadows. Birds sing and butterflies float about on their brilliantly colored wings. How well I remember these scenes – they are the portraits of my childhood.

During the summer, Romania's farmers work very hard. Women, wearing colorful blouses, skirts and head kerchiefs, work beside men garbed in white shirts, dark trousers and hats. Together, they walk to the fields early in the morning and work side by side until sunset. Even today, most Romanian farmers use no machines. Their labor goes on continuously, because most work is done by hand.

During the heat of the summer, fragrant hay is harvested for the animals. Fruit, sweetened by the hot sun, weighs heavily on tree boughs. Thunderstorms echo around the hills and mountains, bringing refreshing rain to the rich soil.

In my recollection, the richest time of the year is always the fall. By this time, most of the crops have been harvested. During these frosty months, careful preparations are made for the long winter. The women begin endless canning while the men take their produce to market. Finally, on the wings of a biting north wind, the cold months arrive.

When deep snows pile up around the farms, the men

busy themselves tending the animals in the barns while their wives take care of the children. The first snows remind everyone that soon the Christmas holidays will begin. My boyhood years were climaxed by annual celebrations of Jesus' birth. In those days groups of men, women and children strolled from house to house singing joyous carols about His coming. Our hearts always swelled with happiness as we thought about the kind of love that would send God's infant Son to be the Savior of the world.

Every family spent days, even weeks, preparing meals, cookies and cakes. Delicious festive foods awaited friends and family who came by to sing. On many occasions the local young people dressed in traditional white and red costumes.

On the night of December 31st the children would fill their pockets with candies and wheat. Laughing with pleasure, they would run throughout the house giving people tastes of the candy, throwing the grain about and wishing everyone prosperity and good crops during the coming year. In spite of the joyless philosophy of communism, these Christian traditions persist.

In the spring come the Easter holidays. Romanians dress in special national costumes lavishly embroidered with flowers. They go to churches carrying with them baskets of different shaped bread loaves, baked cookies, and brightly colored cakes. All these are given in remembrance of the death and resurrection of Jesus Christ.

For centuries, such deeply meaningful celebrations have been respected and loved by Romanians. But since 1947, the Communist Party has worked diligently to destroy Romania's holiday festivities. Why? Because the name of God through Jesus is praised too freely for their atheistic tastes.

When communism came to Romania everything became

the property of the government. People in the big cities were put to work in factories. Their scheduled vacations were taken at various recreational areas. Only then did they enjoy the loveliness of their nation. Our people are hard-working lovers of freedom. Our land once was rich in all kinds of good things; gold mines, coal, minerals, abundant food, pure water and even liberty. But today, because of the government, there is not even enough for each individual to eat. Freedom ceased to exist under communism.

My observation is that, today, most of the people of Romania are very unhappy. Because of their many problems and bad treatment, scores of disillusioned citizens have tried to run away, hoping to emigrate to the United States of America or to other free, non-communist nations. As much as the Romanian people love their country, some have felt they must bid it "goodbye" and move on in search of freedom.

We Christians, of course, look forward to the second coming of Christ. We know that when He returns we will be with Him in heaven rejoicing with all our hearts - truly free at last. Tears will all stop then. We will never say farewell to those we love. We will know no more pain and sorrow. But until then, nearly all Romanian Christians look back at the country they once knew with much sadness and a great sense of loss.

My native village, Hintesti, is located in the Northern part of Romania known as Moldavia, about 18 kilometers from the Russian border. *(The Moldavian area of Russia was part of this same area of Romania until the Russians seized control.)* When I was a boy, it was a wonderfully tranquil place; lush with woods - watered by rivers - sheltered by hills. I was born in a comfortable home with seven spacious rooms. Outside we had a big garden where we grew vegetables, grapes and strawberries. In front and to the side of our home stood an old orchard filled with cherry and apple trees, as well as my father's pride and joy - his beehives.

Our house was situated in the bend of a swiftly flowing river called the Siret. On the shore of the river, hundreds of trees lifted their graceful branches toward heaven.

My family was one that knew God. My father, George Duduman, never failed to call upon the name of the Lord. Dad was a handsome, blonde man with friendly blue eyes. He was born in 1891 and lived until he was 85 years old. My mother's name was Ecaterina (*Catinca*). Like my father, she, too had bright blue eyes. Her hair shone copper red. In the beginning, the two of them shared a quiet, happy life together. They raised seven children; six boys and a girl.

With the deepest love, my parents introduced me to God. They prayed constantly for their children, asking the Lord to make us His servants. My dad's father, Costache, also talked to me about the Lord. He was a fair haired, handsome man who lived to be 115 years old. Very strong all his life, he worked long, hard hours as a forester.

Grandfather lived in the woods about 3 kilometers from our village. It was a tiny community called Beresti. Even now, I can almost see him as he walked toward our home in his spotless white shirt and pants - his cheeks blushing red in the fresh air. He would have his hands behind his back, taking slow but firm steps.

I was always watching, waiting for him. When at last he would come into sight I would shout, "Grandpa is coming! Grandpa is coming!"

Once he saw me, he would kiss me, and ask, "Dumitru, have you been a good boy? Have you been behaving well?"

"Yes, grandpa, I'm always a good boy..."

Then the two of us would sit on the doorstep talking until my parents came home from the fields. Grandpa would place a weathered hand on my head and tell me wonderful stories about God. How I loved to hear about Jesus!

Sometimes, after my parents arrived, he would say, "Children, I think I'm going to sleep here. Night is on its way and it's growing too dark for me to walk home now." My brothers, my sister, and I would be so glad we'd hug his neck and grab him around the waist. Sometimes we'd make a circle around him and sing Christian songs and pray.

Now and then he would take me to his home. Together we would walk to Beresti. There, we'd go into the woods to gather mushrooms, or to hunt rabbits and deer. In the evening we'd pick bouquets of wild flowers for me to take back to Mother.

It was my grandfather who tenderly planted the seeds of faith in my young heart. He served God with love and gentleness until the end of his days. It was because of him, and my father's testimony, that I eventually came to serve the Lord myself. I know without a doubt that someday I will walk with my Grandfather once again.

My father loved working in his orchard, taking care of his bees, tending the garden and fishing. Many times, when he was nearly finished with his work, he'd put his hands on his back, stretch and look up at the sky. "Come help me, Dumitru, because when we're done, we can go fishing!"

What happy words to my young ears! During the summer, Dad used to catch fish with his bare hands. He'd walk into the stream all the way to his waist, closely watching the rippling waters. SNATCH! Out the fish would come! My brothers and I would run along behind, stuffing the fluttering fish into a sack. Once the sack was filled, we'd take all the fish home and fry them for the family to enjoy.

Back then, when I was a young boy, my parents were rich. They had many acres of land and two houses; one in our village and one at the river. In those days it was a sure sign of wealth to have a fireplace oven, and we had one.

Something happened when I was about eight years old that taught us all about true riches; our riches in Jesus. I became very ill. As time went by, I began to suffer more and more discomfort. I'm not sure now what kind of illness it was, but with every passing day I felt as if my life was fading away. At that time in our country there were few doctors, and virtually no medicine. Age-old folk concoctions somewhat numbed the pain, but provided no permanent help. Eventually I grew so skinny and weak that I was unable to dress myself or walk. The end seemed near. The situation was desperate, with little or no hope. My poor parents didn't know what to do.

My Dad was a local pastor. One Tuesday evening he was called by some men from a village called Mindresti, just 9 kilometers from our village, to serve them the Lord's Supper.

"How can we go to Mindresti when our son is so ill?" my mother's voice shook with emotion. "We're better off staying here and praying."

"Let's go to Mindresti to pray with the Brothers and Sisters there." Dad's voice grew quieter, "Can't you see that he's dying? It's better that we go and pray for him."

When my parents arrived in Mindresti, they shared my hopeless situation with the other Christians. With one voice, they all began to pray for my life. After a time of prayer, a prophecy came forth; "Do not fear! The Lord has touched Dumitru and has healed him!"

Everyone rejoiced and thanked God. After the service was over, my mother and father rushed to their horse cart, and raced home. To their wonder and joy, they found me walking, full of energy, and thanking God for what He had done.

God was surely the only physician who could have healed me. I was just a small child, and yet I felt His mighty power. In all of this, I came to understand that God loves me! I still praise Him for His goodness to me in that time.

After that, I began to go to school. There was religious persecution in Romania even then. Because I was a Christian, the teacher beat me and sent me home time after time. It was very hard to continue going to school. My situation brought sadness and pain to my parents. They cried out to God day and night asking Him to help us in this matter. Even though there was no answer at that time, I can see now that those circumstances were permitted by God to strengthen us all. Various forms of religious suppression were growing more and more common in those days.

The Nazis came in 1941, and with them the sorrows of persecution. It wasn't long, before the Gestapo authorities were arresting true believers and hustling them off to prison.

My father was a good Christian - a God fearing man - even though faith and belief were very unpopular. The first one who really suffered in our family was Dad, beginning in the spring of 1941. Because he was the pastor of our village church, and those of surrounding villages, a close eye was kept on him.

One day when he was praying with some other Christians he was caught by the police - some very violent police! They arrested him and beat him up; pounding his head, stomach and ribs! They stomped on him! They hit him with their shotguns! They squeezed his fingers in the door!

The Nazis took him to court before a black-robed judge who wore a cynical expression on his face and openly made fun of God. With eyes as cold as steel, he sentenced George

8

Duduman, the father of seven children, to twenty-five years in prison!

When the verdict was given, there was a moment of horrified silence in the courtroom, broken by my mother's desperate cry. "It's okay, Ecaterina," my father called to her from behind the railing across the crowded room. "Don't cry. If I never return, God will help you when the hard times..."

He never finished. He was silenced by the guard's fist as he yelled, "How dare you talk about God here!"

"God have mercy on you," my father answered boldly, "and make you a Christian."

The next person brought to trial was a godly woman named Anna. She was about 85 years old. The judge's bitter voice proclaimed Anna's sentence, "Old woman, you are sentenced to twenty-five years in prison. Do you think you will live that long?"

Softly she replied, "Your Honor, the years I cannot finish you will finish in my place." The judge laughed uproariously.

That evening at home, my mother said, "Boys, you no longer have a father. Only God can get your father out of prison."

Nine months later, the Russian army invaded Romania. Soon, everything happened just as old Anna had prophesied. The Christians were released from their prisons. The Nazi officials who had put them there, including that particular judge, were imprisoned. For a couple of years, Christians lived free without fear. But this relief was short-lived. By 1947, the communist party had become extremely strong. Soon the struggle faced by Christian believers was even greater than it had been under Hitler.

Of course my father came home, but his difficulties

were by no means over. When the communist persecutions first began, some Christian Brothers and Sisters began to inform the authorities against other believers. This soon became less successful for the KGB, because the Spirit of God began to point out those who were doing the informing. When the Spirit's work against the Communist informers in the church became known to the authorities, a much stronger front was formed against the Christians; particularly those who practiced the miraculous gifts of the Holy Spirit in their churches. Hardships for believers sharply increased.

One day two police officers came to our home wearing crisp blue uniforms. They strutted into the yard with shotguns in their hands. "Where is your father?" one of them barked.

"He's inside, eating," I answered, trembling.

"Go tell him who's outside," the officer said smugly.

Hot tears burned our faces as we watched them take him away. He was placed in a big prison in the city of Dorohoi, where once again he was violently beaten. There he was commanded to become a member of the Communist Party. He was ordered to convince other Christians in his church to do the same. But George Duduman was strengthened by the hand of God. No matter how cruelly he was tortured, he never gave up.

Meanwhile, my brother, Costache, was also arrested. He was sentenced to one and a half years in a Bucharest prison. This prison is built over the Dimbovita river. There, he was kept in a cell where the floors were nothing more than metal grates, with the frigid river waters flowing beneath. Because of the brutal cold and endless humidity, disease attacked his feet. He suffered greatly the rest of his life, having lost one foot and all of the toes on the other. Severe pain made it very difficult for him to walk.

(In April, 1990, God allowed me to visit my brother once again - after a 6 year separation! His last words to me were, "I prayed to God and asked Him to let me live long enough to see you one more time. Now that my prayers have been answered, I can die in peace." Less than 3 weeks later - eleven days after I returned to America - he died.)

Although the rest of the family was not arrested, we were ordered to hard labor in the communist farmlands. This lasted for six years. School had become a nightmare. We were given no future because of our faith. I was an excellent student, and graduated at the top of my class. Despite my diligence, I was told that I couldn't go on to seek a higher education because I was the son of a Christian. "No matter how good you are," the educational authorities told me, "you cannot be received in our school." I lost heart upon hearing these words.

From age fourteen to seventeen I helped my parents work, but I grew more and more depressed. I was wandering from God. But I wasn't the only one. My brothers were drifting, too. Instead of our troubles drawing us closer to our Heavenly Father, we were deliberately pushing ourselves away.

In their anxiety and heartache, my parents began to cry out for the Lord to have mercy. "Bring our sons back to You!" they pleaded. Day after day, my father wept, praying fervently, singing out each name. "God have mercy on Dumitru. Father, forgive Alexandru. Lord, help Vasile, save Corneliu, and turn Costache and Elena back to You."

As He always does, the Lord had mercy. He forgave. He brought help in answer to those tear-bathed prayers. But the years to come were not easy ones; and the road was rough and hard.

MY BELOVED GRANDFATHER, COSTACHE

Chapter Two

PRAYERS AND PROMISES

My dear parents! How my angry rejection of God darkened my seventeenth year for them. I was inducted into the Romanian Army and their hearts were grieved as they observed my cocky, ambitious behavior. My first tour of duty was boot camp in Chitila. For eight months I was challenged by this very demanding training program. The work there could only be described as rough, hard and dirty.

When the eight months finally ended, we celebrated with a huge festival in the nation's capital, Bucharest. Our squad took part in this military display. The commanders selected a special group of men to march who were approximately the same height. How proud I was to find myself one of them. Dressed in our crisp uniforms, we participated in the first such parade ever to pass through the streets of Romania's capital.

After the parade, the best soldiers were sent to Constanta Military School. Once again, I was among them. I was delighted because I wouldn't have to work hard labor any more. Better yet, success at this school would provide me with a pleasant future. I started at Constanta in 1951 and stayed there four and a half years. I flourished at

13

military school. I strutted with pride in my black and white uniform, fully appreciating the less militant tone of my commanders. We often took trips down the Mamaia Ghiol River for training and experience.

At the end of my schooling, I received the diploma of Lieutenant in the Marines (a branch of the Army). I soon had eighty soldiers under my command. They liked me and would listen to me.

We were stationed on the Black Sea at Constanta. One day I received an order from the Communist Commander to search every ship coming into the harbor from foreign countries. The order was: if I should find Bibles, I was to confiscate them and arrest the missionaries. "If you cooperate in this we will award you with a higher rank," my superior officers promised.

I received these orders with pleasure, quite sure that I would accomplish the confiscations and thus advance myself quickly. I aggressively began searching the foreign vessels. One morning a ship steamed into harbor from Holland. Sensing success, I took eight of my soldiers with me. We began an exhaustive search. Finally, under some boxes of cookies, I came upon some Bibles. When I saw them I was ecstatic. "They're going to give me a couple of stars for my shoulder!" I thought. "Nobody can compete with me!"

I called harshly to the Dutch captain, "Whose Bibles are these?"

"I don't know," he shrugged.

"Don't worry," I barked, "you'll know, all right, or you won't leave this port!" Just then, glancing to my right, I noticed a tall man standing. He was crying and I saw he was moving his lips.

"This fellow is praying!" I said to myself. "These must be his Bibles!" I went to him and demanded his passport. He gave it to me. "Are these your Bibles?" I inquired.

14

"No..."

"Well then, whose are they?" My voice was growing louder with each question, so much was I enjoying my authority.

"They are your Brothers' and Sisters'," the man quietly answered, looking directly into my eyes.

When I heard him, it was as if someone had stabbed me in the heart. Suddenly my mind was filled with the memory that my father was a pastor and my Brothers were Christians. What had I become?

Then I heard a voice say, "Dumitru, what are you doing? I brought you here. Don't confiscate the Bibles. Return the man's passport and help him unload the Bibles. If you don't do as I say I will punish you!"

I looked around to see the person talking to me, and was embarrassed to see no one. I rushed into another compartment, but the voice was even louder in there. I put my fingers in my ears but it was even louder. I was trembling and could not stop. I new it was the Lord talking to me.

I went back with the man's documents in my hand, shaking like a leaf in the wind. "Here's your passport," I said. "God has heard your prayers."

When he heard me he stared at me in astonishment. "You are going to become a Christian!" He exclaimed.

"Shut up," I ordered, "or I will arrest you! NOW - I will provide you with some soldiers to help you unload the Bibles and to protect you from the police." And with that I turned on my heel, leaving him standing in amazement.

Once I had given him his passport back, I didn't hear the voice any more. I was gripped with fear realizing that only the voice of the Lord could speak to me like that.

I thought in my heart that God had brought me there to protect the Bibles coming into the country. The

15

Communist government didn't tell me to look for guns or rockets. Only Bibles. *(Which one do they think is the more powerful weapon?)*

For two years I remained on the Black sea, able to lend a hand to the missionaries; enabling them to import their precious cargos of Bibles. Then I was sent to officers school. After six months I returned to my unit as a major.

Unexpectedly, the Communist government of Romania issued an order which was to change my life forever. When I returned to my unit, I was called into the office of the General. "I'm sorry Dumitru," he said. "You are a good man and I like you, but after tomorrow you will no longer work here."

"Why?" was all I could ask as my heart sank.

"The government has ordered that all soldiers in the Romanian Army who are Christians or come from Christian homes be sent home. I am sorry, Dumitru, there is nothing I can do."

There I was, all of twenty-four years old. I had put my trust in my ability and intelligence; now, all at once I was being sent back to my parents!

Anger seethed within me. As I caught the first train home I bitterly decided to take revenge on my father. After all, it was their fault I was kicked out of the Army!

When I arrived home, my mother looked at me in absolute surprise.

"What are you doing home, Dumitru?" she asked. "What is wrong with you? Why are you so upset?"

"Because of your Christianity they kicked me out of the army!" I spat the words at her. "Where is Dad?"

"At the church," she meekly answered.

"I'm going to go there and embarrass him!"

"Hold on," she said reaching for my arm. "He'll be home soon."

16

"No!" I pulled away. "I'm going there, NOW and and take revenge for what he has done to me!"

I rushed to the church, planning to take my revenge quickly. As I approached the church, I heard a most beautiful song about the Good Shepherd searching for the one lost sheep. I knew that lost sheep was me! I started to cry.

Once inside, I *quietly* slipped in beside my father. "Why am I crying?" I asked him.

"Be quiet," he answered. "I'll tell you after the service."

At the end of the service my father stood up and joyfully announced, "Brethren, our prayers have been answered! After four and a half years of prayer, Dumitru has been dismissed from the military! Now, I pray that God will make him a soldier in HIS army!"

Everyone began to pray and thank God for hearing their prayers. While they were praying, one of the Brother's began to prophecy in a loud voice. "Because you have protected my workers, I will protect you. I have chosen you out of the world to be my servant."

I became frightened. I knew that I would be thrown in prison if anyone found out what I had done with regards to the Bibles and missionaries.

"Who told him what I did?" I hoarsely questioned my father.

"Nobody. This prophesy was a revelation from the Holy Spirit," he explained. He went on to say that if I would listen to God and do what the Bible teaches, God WOULD make me a commander in His heavenly army. "What you have lost now is nothing compared to what God will give you later. Don't be sad."

At that time two ideas were struggling within me. Should I give my life to God, or not? Torn between

17

conflicting worlds, I made no choice at that time, but I realized that relations between God and me were not very good and what Dad had said was true.

Not long after my return home, I decided that I wanted to get married. Young people in our country at that time asked their parents' opinion as to whom they should marry. When I talked to my Dad he suggested I marry one of the girls in the church. But I complained by saying that they were too poor. Then he told me, "Marry a rich girl if you want; just give your heart to the Lord."

I asked my father how he felt about me marrying Maria Tipu. He said Maria was a fine, hard-working girl, but reminded me that she was poorer then the girls in the church, because she was a widow's daughter. (Her father, having gone to World War II under the Nazi occupation, was reportedly taken prisoner by the Russians and never heard from again.)

Having my father's approval, I began dating her.

Because Maria was the oldest of three girls, she was the one on whom her mother depended. Our courtship was marred with misunderstandings between Maria, her mother and me. But before long we were joyfully married. Our wedding took place on the 21st of May, 1956. It was a sunny day - the fruit trees heavy with pink and white blossoms. We had only a little money, a cow, a horse, and a small piece of ground that our parents gave us. We lived in the same house with my parents, but went often to help Maria's mother in the field.

My father tried, with words of love and gentleness, to explain to Maria the way of God, and how important it is to have faith in Him. Maria's family knew nothing about the Kingdom of God.

After a year we had our first baby - a little girl that we named Virginia, born April 18, 1957. We were overwhelmed with happiness and loved her so dearly.

It is against the law for doctors to make home deliveries in Romania and the mother is supposed to be taken by ambulance to the hospital several miles away, but because the doctor was a friend and knew us well, he delivered Virginia at the dispensary which was close to our home. God performed many favors to His people in spite of the harassments by the government. The doctor was a Communist.

Just one year later Maria gave birth to a baby boy and we named him Costica. He was born October 28, 1958. We were so happy, seeing that he was especially cute and smart. But when he was only five and a half months old he died. This was a great tragedy for us. We hoped for some time that we would have another child, then we learned that Maria would be unable to bear any more children.

This news tore me apart and, like never before in my life, I realized that I needed God's comfort. No one else could reach the ache in my heart. We both felt we needed God more than anything else and decided to begin attending church. The next Sunday we dressed nicely and walked to a nearby church service. We were received by everyone there with an outpouring of sincere love. Everyone welcomed us.

After the messages from the Lord had been given, we stood up and told the congregation that we wanted to serve God. "We are so happy for you!" the pastor said. He beamed with pleasure. Then he turned to the people and said, "Let us rejoice and all sing together, 'I have Decided To Follow Jesus'."

Not many days later we were baptized in water. Then I began to fast and pray to be filled with the Holy Spirit.

My love for the Lord continued to grow daily. The day finally when I was actually filled with His Spirit. I still say that was the happiest day of my life. My whole being was overcome with joy; I couldn't thank Him enough for this miraculous work of His Son.

Soon I began to preach the Word. I preached wherever there were church services. (In Romania there is more than one speaker in a service.)

Not long after I gave my heart to God, He began using me. People were coming to Christ. Some were being healed and others were filled with the Holy Ghost. Much of what God did was through much fasting and prayer. God was at work, and the enemy didn't like it.

Then Maria became ill! Something was wrong with her eyes. When I asked her what happened, she said that while working in the fields, a bit of "horse tail" grass had lodged in one eye. The ensuing infection soon spread to both eyes.

The problem first appeared as a white membrane. It grew until it covered her entire eyes from the outside corner and continued across the pupils until she became almost blind. Her eyelids were inflamed all the time. Her head hurt and her eyes ached.

"God," I cried out, "I gave my life to you and now my Maria can't see. Why?"

I took her to a good doctor; an older man. He told us she would never see again unless God healed her. I didn't believe him, so I took her to many other specialists. Whenever I would hear of another one, away we went. Unfortunately nothing they did or gave her provided any relief. I spent all my savings from the military going from doctor to doctor. little by little I became very despondent. Before long I couldn't preach. I couldn't pray. Seeing my despair, my father came to me and I began to weep, pouring out my agony and heartbreak over Maria.

"I've let you go your own way to see what you would do, Son," he told me with kindness flickering in his blue eyes. "Now, why don't you try my doctor?"

"Who?" I asked.

My father simply said, "Jesus."

"You don't understand!" I raged. "Everyone is mocking and laughing at me saying, 'Can't you see that since you became a Christian your wife became ill? The medicines only make her worse.' I don't know what to do!"

"Dumitru don't listen to what people say to you. You believe in a great God."

"Well, what AM I supposed to do?!"

"We will fast and pray and believe God together." More than forty of us joined together in fasting and prayer. A few weeks later a Brother named Vasile Munteanu came on his bike from about 30 kilometers away to see me. He said, "I was on my way to a prayer meeting, but the Holy Spirit told me to come and take you with me."

"I'd love to go, but I'll have to ask Maria if she would mind staying alone for a few hours."

I told Maria about the prayer meeting and she said, "Go, but pray for me, too." I got my bike and went with him.

The village we were going to was on the Russian border and difficult to enter because of the check point where everyone was searched for Bibles being carried into Russia.

As we rode along, we worried about how we would get through. But this time we were not searched! When we arrived at the service the pastor said, "Welcome Brothers, the Holy Spirit told us you were coming, so we prayed for your protection." Then the pastor said "What is your name?"

"Dumitru Duduman."

He said, "Brother Duduman, the Lord told us that your wife is sick and today he is going to heal her. I have had a vision of a blond woman with blue eyes, lying on a table. A man dressed in white was beside the table preparing to operate on her eyes."

A great joy came over me! Could it be true?

"This is what the Lord says, Brother Duduman. 'I have listened to your prayers and I have seen your fasting. Beginning today, your wife will be able to see'." How I praised God for this! All the church joined me in thanking God and praying for my wife.

At the end of the service Brother Ursulica asked me to pray. As I started to pray, I suddenly felt a remarkable surge of power and I had a vision; a big globe of light was over me. It burned brightly, blazing with golden light. Then suddenly it exploded and out of it came shafts of light. One of these beams came inside me while the other shining beams went into those who prayed with me. At the same time this was happening, God began to speak through a Brother. "Young man!" he proclaimed. "Listen to God's word, for in this day I have put great power inside you and have decided to make you one of My workers. I want to use you in an unusual ministry which you do not comprehend now, but you will understand later. As a sign that I will do this, I have touched your wife. When you get home she will be waiting for you at the gate and will open it for you. Her eyesight will have been restored and she will have food on the table for you."

Again I poured out my thanks to God, then told the Brothers what I had seen. As soon as the service was over, I started for the door. Brother Ursulica, the pastor, asked, "Where are you going?"

"I'm going home to see if my wife is healed."

"I'm going with you, to see if what the Holy Ghost has said is true." Brother Ursulica said.

He accompanied me as I rushed home to see what God

had done. There was no doubt in my heart as to what I would find. After riding our bicycles an hour and a half over winding country roads, we neared the house and I saw Maria leaning on the gate. As we came close she shouted, "I can see! I can see!"

We left our bikes at the fence and, jumping over it, I ran to Maria. Looking into her eyes I could see that they were as clear as the day I married her. I fell on my knees and gave God thanks. Then we hurried on into the house to see if the food was prepared. Of course it was. "Maria, what happened?" I asked.

She laughed with joy and said, "I was in bed, and for some reason I was praising and thanking the Lord... I don't know why! All at once I was thrust out of bed and onto my knees. Then I heard the door open and I saw - yes saw - your Dad enter! It was about 9:00 this morning..."

I quickly calculated that this was the same hour the Lord had spoken to me.

"When he came in," she continued, "I got up and began saying, 'Dad, I can see!'."

After our meal we prayed with Brother Ursulica and thanked God for His wonderful work that He had done. From that day on my wife has had no more trouble with her eyes.

This was the first lesson I learned after I came to the Lord - and it was a critical one for my continuing walk with Him. It was this: **whenever we pass through problems, we should immediately call upon God. No matter what our circumstances, this is the kind of relationship that He wants with us - for He knows that this instant dependency can only bring us closer to Him.**

I tried to fast and pray more, because I believed that in so doing, the Lord would give me more power to do His work.

One day I had a vision. I saw a tall, handsome man dressed in white. He spoke to me saying, "Behold, man! I've come to tell you that you are being prepared for a special ministry. You have been gifted with the Holy Spirit and have received new life. You have been filled with power. Don't stop seeking the face of the Lord. You cannot understand everything now, but you will understand later on. Very, very soon the work will begin."

After this the man disappeared. I continued to pray, and said to God, "Do as You wish with my life! I trust in Your powerful hands. You are free to do as You want with me..."

I hadn't even finished saying these words, and again the messenger appeared to me. "I am the Chief Commander of the Heavenly Army and I have come to tell you more good news. Come fasting and praying before God, and through you the prayers of many Christians will be fulfilled. Don't fear that you will not be able to do what you're asked because of its difficulty. The Lord will teach you all you need to know."

I shook and started to cry. "Lord," I said, "what kind of work or ministry do You have for me?"

The messenger responded, "You will provide Bibles to Christians. You will pass through countless problems and troubles with many days of suffering, but the Lord will be with you and will help you conquer everything."

After all this I had to stop a moment in order to grasp the angel's astonishing appearance and prophetic words. All I could respond was, "Do as You will with me, Lord! I put my trust in You!"

I wondered how I would get Bibles to Christians who needed them. In our country there were no foreigners, and I had no friends in other countries. I didn't know the names of the missionaries I had helped in earlier years and it was impossible even to talk to a person from another country about such matters. If a person were caught in that kind of conversation, he could be imprisoned. Yet in spite of my many unspoken questions, I said, "I know, Lord, that everything You've said is true and nothing will remain unfulfilled." How could I question such a clear and direct message from heaven?

Sometimes it may seem to us that God should fulfill His promises immediately upon giving them, but everything has its season. *"The vision is yet for an appointed time,"* the Bible says. That is why if we have a promise from the Lord and it hasn't yet come to pass, we shouldn't lose hope.

Our responsibility is simply to wait. Any word spoken by the Lord has already been decided by Him. It will most certainly come to pass.

It wasn't long before the Lord gave me clear directions in a dream. He told me where to go and who to see about smuggling Bibles from Western Europe into Romania. Soon, by obeying the Word of the Lord, I knew how to obtain Bibles I would need for distribution.

Of course there was a great deal more to be revealed, but just as He had told me, the Lord was going to use me to answer the prayers of innumerable Christian Brothers and Sisters. I would be the one privileged to place the priceless Word of God into their outstretched hands!

MYSELF AS AN ARMY OFFICER

- left to right -
CORNELIU (my brother), ME, VIRGINIA (my daughter),
MARIA (my wife), CATINCA (my Mother)

Chapter Three

GOD'S SPECIAL MESSENGER

Romania is a rich and fertile land. I always found pleasure and profit in working the soil and seeing it bring forth its fruit. In those days, the journeys I made to sell my farm produce allowed me to visit Christians in various village churches - preaching, praying and working with them.

As I traveled from church to church, I quickly noticed that most people had no Bibles. My visitation from the angel never left my thoughts. Men and women would ask to borrow my Bible in order to copy verses from it. There might be one Bible in the whole church, so treasured verses were written on pieces of paper. This broke my heart, and I began wishing that the words of the angel would quickly come to pass. But how would God make it possible for me to furnish these Christians with God's word? I had no contacts with any foreigners. The missionaries that I had met did not give me their names or addresses. All of this troubled me greatly. As I puzzled over this dilemma one night I had a powerful dream.

In this lengthy night vision, the Lord told me just how to find Bibles and what to do to get them distributed to the right people.

27

He told me to return to The Black Sea and go to work for the officer I had served under while in the military... but this time as a civilian. There, He would show me what to do. In the process of this I would make arrangements for places of storage, and means of eventually distributing the Bibles.

I returned to The Black Sea and went to my old commander. I said, "Sir, I have married, I don't have a Job, and am unable to care for my family. I am willing to take a job - no matter how bad it is." He said, "I can't have you working here. You used to be one of my officers."

"But I need the work. Don't you have something I can do?"

"No! I don't have any jobs for Christians!"

"At least, let me be a trash cleaner."

"No! I can't see you with a broom in you're hand."

"But, what AM I supposed to do?

"Can you cook?" he asked.

"Sure," I quickly replied.

"Go to the officers mess hall and tell them I sent you. They will put you to work."

And so it was that I worked there for two months, serving those who I used to command. They constantly made fun of me and spit on me. I had to tell myself, "Have patience, Dumitru," because Christ had more patience than I could ever have.

One day while we were preparing a meal, an officer came in and announced, "Ships are coming from Holland! Let's go search for Bibles!"

When he said that, I heard the familiar voice in my ear say, "Hurry! Deig is coming!" I left everything and ran to the ship. (Brother Dieg was the same man whom I had first encountered before I knew the Lord.)

My father had assured me that all the Bibles that I had

allowed to come in to the country had been distributed, but were later confiscated by the government. Now, because of my dream, I knew that Brother Dieg would once again come into my life. Sure enough, as I stood waiting, he walked off the ship with his overcoat over his arm.

"Peace of the Lord, Brother Dieg!" I quietly said to him. When he saw me in civilian clothes, tears filled his eyes. "What has happened?" he whispered. I told him to meet me at a certain hotel in Constanta. We both knew that we dared not be seen talking. If caught talking to a foreigner, I knew I could receive at least a six month jail sentence, and up to as much as four years.

He went one way and I went another. Later we met at the hotel. He carefully locked the room door and I shared my heart with him.

I never returned to my job. Brother Dieg and I traveled to Bucharest to meet Brother Andrew of "Open Doors", Harlan Popoff of "Door of Hope", Brother Wurmbrandt and other missionaries, who's names I did not know at the time. Here we entered into an agreement as to how the Bibles would be handled. Not many weeks later, I was called to Bucharest by my friends there. I did not wait for them to call twice but caught the first train out. When I arrived at my friend's home, there among them was Brother Dieg! The Brothers began to introduce us. Brother Dieg began to laugh when someone asked who I was. He told them that I was the one God had used to work with Bibles before, when they gave Bibles to Romania. The brethren said, "We asked God about you, whether He wanted you to be part of this ministry or not. He said you can be trusted. We want you to know that you can come and get Bibles from us anytime you want to." Dieg and I embraced, tears of laughter and joy streaming down our faces. That was also when I found out who all the other Brothers were.

For four years, Bibles came into Romania Freely. Then the borders began to close and it became very hard to get the Word of God into the country. I knew all too well how deeply the Communists fear the Word of God... they fear it more than anything else. As a Marine, it had not been guns, weapons or contraband I had been ordered to search for... only Bibles!

Months passed. Harvest time returned and Maria and I went to Ialomita, some 600 kilometers away from our village, with potatoes to trade for wheat. One september morning I was going to the mill to pick up my wheat when a soldier carrying a shotgun appeared before me and thrust his weapon into my chest. "Where are you going?" he asked. "You must leave everything behind and go to Constanta! And don't worry," the messenger went on, "The Lord will take care of everything. Through you, He wants to provide an answer for seventy Christians who are praying and fasting."

I gasped for breath and turned around, rushing back to the house where I had left Maria. Brother Tache was at the house, a man who had been my friend long before I became a Christian. Everyone was startled to see me coming back so quickly.

"What's wrong, Dumitru?" Maria whispered, her pretty face troubled.

"Nothing is wrong..." I began shaking my head. "It's just that the angel of the Lord stopped me and told me to leave everything here and go to Constanta."

When Brother Tache heard this, he said, "Let's go back to the place where you saw the angel. I want to see him, too!"

We returned to the same location and there was the soldier again, but this time he stopped me with a sword in my chest.

30

"I told you to go to Constanta." His voice was stern. "Where are you going now? If you will not go this time, I will punish you with sickness!"

As he disappeared, Brother Tache's words were almost inaudible.

"You better go to Constanta right now, Dumitru. You simply cannot fool around with God. If it will make it any easier for you, I will go with you."

We returned to the house and got ready to go, taking our wives with us. In spite of our hurry, we missed the bus that would take us to the train. Just as I was wondering why the angel couldn't have held up the bus, a car pulled up. "Hurry and get in so we don't miss your train," the driver said. Puzzled but desperate, the four of us climbed into the car. The driver didn't even ask us where we were going. We traveled so fast from Fetesti to Unirea, a 30 kilometer drive that we didn't even have time to think. He jumped out at the station, got our tickets and handed them to us. When we tried to pay him, he said, "Forget it. You're going to miss your train." He walked away, and as I turned to thank him, he and his car were gone... they seemed to have disappeared!

Once on the train, we agreed that surely an angel of the Lord had once again appeared to us. As we rode along, my thoughts raced ahead of us to Constanta. What would we do once we got there? Then all at once I heard the angel's voice, and he appeared. "Didn't I tell you not to worry?" he said. "I said that the Lord would take care of everything. Now I'm here to tell you what to expect when you arrive. Wait in front of the station until a man arrives and inquires, 'Who doesn't know anybody here?' You will say, 'I am the one who doesn't know anybody.' Go with that man because he will be sent by the Lord to help you. Trust in God and don't be afraid because everything I have told you

31

will happen."

When he left me I was full of joy and new courage. I told my wife and friends, who had not seen him, what he had said. Wonderfully excited, we began to sing songs. We arrived in Constanta praising the Lord together.

When we got off the train, our eyes searched the area for the man who was to meet us. Soon he arrived. Our conversation was exactly as the angel had foretold. "Peace of God be with you!" he said, once he realized who we were. "Welcome to Constanta!"

We shook hands. "My name is Ionica Culea, and I am part of the Baptist Church." He invited us to his house and explained warmly how much he would like for us to be his house guests as long as we were in town. We all traveled together on a local bus which stopped right in front of his house.

As we disembarked, we noticed an old woman waiting at the gate. She opened it and invited us in. She was Ionica's 84 year-old mother. After we entered the house we all knelt down and prayed. Then I told the family what had happened regarding the angel. When I finished, the mother, Sister Rada said, "I saw the angel, too. He told me you were coming. He said I should send my son to pick you up. Thank God! Everything He showed me and told me has come true!"

While we were visiting, Brother Ionica said, "Since God has sent you here, I would like you to come with me to pray for a Brother who has cancer. We have been praying for him for a long time."

I said, "Lets pray first, and see what GOD has to say about it." While we were praying, God gave me a word of prophecy for Brother Ionica: "You are the one who needs healing. And you are asking for healing for someone else? I have decided to heal YOU today. You must believe with all of your heart!'"

I anointed him with oil, and we prayed for him. (He had diabetes and migraine headaches.) God healed him instantly! During the rest of his life he had various other physical problems, but NEVER diabetes or migraine headaches!

After Brother Ionica was healed he pressured me to come with him to pray for the man with cancer. On the way to the man's home, God showed me the man had committed adultery. He said if the man would confess his sins, He would heal him. If not, he would die!

When we arrived, I said, "If you confess your sin, God will heal you. If not, you will die in three days!" He refused to confess. Three days later he died.

God continued to work in the hearts of the people in the Baptist Church. Their walk with God has continued to grow in power and faith since that time.

Along with our hosts, we enjoyed a brief tour of the beautiful resort city of Constanta, visiting the aquarium and port. The next morning we found our way to a meeting at a pentecostal church, five kilometers away. We were to get together with a group of Baptists who believed in the work of the Holy Spirit. (As far as I was concerned, it didn't matter what name they bore as long as they believed in the Lord.) That day was especially blessed by the Lord... His Spirit was felt all over the church. After the services, we talked for awhile, and with the Lord's help I was able to give the right answers to their questions. Then we prayed together and our Lord displayed His power to them. He revealed secrets, encouraged hearts and healed the sick. Surely it was in response to the prayers of these faithful ones, that God had sent us to Constanta.

One man among them named Andrei was afflicted with leprosy. He entered the room while we were praying and almost immediately the Holy Spirit spoke to him saying, "Listen, I have chosen to heal you today! If you will wholeheartedly believe, you will be healed of your leprosy at this very moment!"

After we finished praying, Andrei shouted in a loud voice, "Christian friends, I want you to share my happiness! God is so good! Just now he has touched me and healed me of my leprosy!" Andrei's joy was indescribable. He cried and yelled all at the same time.

"You can't imagine how much terror that horrible sickness has brought into my family," he finally explained. "I'm just 28 years old and have been married only a short time. My wife and I were so happy until this leprosy began. Then tragedy came, and I started going from one doctor to another, thinking it was some sort of a sickness that could be cured. Once I realized what it was, I was told that I would have to leave my family and go to a leper colony for the rest of my life. But now the nightmare is over! I am well again!"

"Are you sure you are completely healed?" I asked him.

"I will go to the doctor tomorrow for a full examination," Andrei promised. The healing was confirmed by the puzzled doctors. How we praised God for His goodness! We stayed in that community seven days. The fellowship that we had with the Brothers there was very special. God also used me in miraculous healings, and through that, many came to God. By that time we were anxious and excited to return to our daughter Virginia, who had stayed with my parents in our absence.

After our visit to Constanta, more and more of the Baptist believers began to receive the Holy Spirit. And even as this blessing occurred, the enemy of our souls was hard at work. Unfaithfulness and doubts gripped the hearts of many, and they found themselves betraying their Christian brethren.

By 1961 the government had such control of everything that they forced the people to sign over their land, leaving only a small plot for the individual. We were forced to work in the fields so the government could have the crops to sell to the foreign countries for State revenue. I didn't have money to buy food and clothes and we were becoming ill. My wife, daughter and I worked in the fields with no compensation from daylight until dark. Jobs were hard to find. Maria and I began to pray and fast to God about the situation. One day, as we worked in the fields, three men dressed in green uniforms came to us and said, "We understand you are a good hunter and have some military background. We need a good, reliable man at the post as warden. If you think you would like to have the job, we will hire you." I accepted the job gladly because it was God's answer to our prayers. I worked there for twelve years. God supplied money for me and my family and I had money to help others. I was also able to give them Bibles. I had devoted my life completely to God's work.

I didn't realize it then, but my troubles were just beginning. The communist agents began to watch me step by step.

I was called back to Constanta by the Brothers. When I arrived, there was already a group gathered in prayer. There were many sick people in the group.

Emil and Vlad wore glasses with the strongest magnification possible. Silvica had a very serious skin infection all over her body. No matter what she tried, it never got better. Then there was Taina, who was born blind.

We sang a few songs first. The power of the Holy Spirit was so powerful the building almost shook! Then we prayed

35

for everyone at once. During the prayer, God opened Taina's eyes. She said, "I can see! I can see!"

When we finished praying, Taina said, "What am I going to do if God doesn't allow me to keep my eyesight?" Immediately, when she spoke her doubt, she lost her eyesight, and has never regained it until today!

At the same time - throwing away his glasses - Emil begin crying out, "Thank you God, for healing me!" He picked up a Bible, went outside and began reading it in the moonlight.

Vlad threw down his glasses and stomped them, as he praised God for his healing.

Silvica was on her knees, crying an praising God. Her skin was as clear as a baby's skin.

As I stated before, when the work of the Lord began to flourish, then came envy and jealousy. One person was Pastor Duduica. He began to fight the work and went to the authorities.

While I was there the Holy Spirit warned me about this man. He had gone to the authorities saying, "There is a man who is responsible for the new movement. He is a troublemaker among the people of my church. His name is Dumitru Duduman."

The Holy Spirit was quick to give me directions regarding this unsettling turn of events. He instructed me one morning, "Go to the Duduica home and wait there until he comes home. If you go there you will not be found by the Secret Police." Telling the other Brothers what God had shown me, we decided to fast and pray together.

I got out of bed that morning and dressed quickly, then headed for Pastor Duduica's house. Only his wife and children were there. When she saw me, she was very angry. As I entered the house I said, "The peace of the Lord be with you!"

36

"My husband is not here," stammered his wife.

"Oh, that's all right. I'll just sit here and wait for him."
I sat down and began to read my Bible. I didn't say any
more to her - just waited for her husband to come. As
darkness came, I wondered how long it would be. I was
feeling a little uncomfortable waiting there for such a long
time. Nevertheless, I stayed, feeling the Lord's direction to
remain. I just kept reading the scriptures. Finally, about
1:00 a.m., the door opened and Pastor Duduica entered.
When he saw me in his own home he turned ghostly white
and demanded, "What are you doing here?" falling down,
by the door full of fright.

I went over to him and told him to get up - that the
Holy Spirit told me that he was looking for me with the
Secret Police, going to different houses of the Brothers.
"The Lord said if I came to your house you wouldn't search
here for me."

Tears filled the man's eyes. "It is true, I went with the
Secret Police to the homes of all your friends. It never
occurred to me that you would come here to my house."

He looked at me for a moment and then began to cry.
"I can see that the One who watches over you is far more
capable than the Secret Police. I am sorry that I struggled
like a crazy man against you. Now I can see that you are
indeed led by the Holy Spirit. Please forgive me, Brother!"

"Pastor Duduica, God needs to forgive you. You were
fighting against Him, not against me."

"Let's make a deal," he said. "I know someone in my
church who has committed adultery. Tomorrow night we
will go to church, and if God is *really* with you, He will
show you who this man is." I agreed, knowing that God
always gave me victory.

With that, I excused myself and returned to my friends
that night. I told them what had happened, and also told

37

them to continue to pray with me. The next evening Pastor Duduica and I went to church. As we entered the church, I stopped and told the pastor, "Do you see the man on the right side of the pulpit, he is the one you were referring to." Would you like me to call all those who have the same sin up here," I asked? "No thank you," he said, "I have seen enough. Now I KNOW that God is guiding you."

Afterwards he introduced me to the church and said I was going to be the one who would lead the service that night. I felt, through the power that was over me, God had work to do that night.

That evening, as I was standing before them, I began to tell them I hadn't come to change anything, but that I prayed for God to do the changes in all of us. After we praised God with a few songs, we read a word and began to pray one by one. The first prayed, the second, and the third. When the fourth began to pray, a power came over the whole church and all of them began to pray. Seventy people received the Holy Spirit that evening and everyone felt the power of God except the pastor, who was trying to stop the prayer. How we rejoiced, seeing that God had solved the problem of the Christians in Constanta. I remembered how God had sent me there in the first place... how mighty His plans had been, even though I hadn't been able to see the outcome when I first left my own business and obeyed Him!

As I was leaving, the Holy Spirit led me to go to Bucharest. I wondered, "What will I do in Bucharest?"

I arrived at the home of a friend, and had no more than entered the room when the doorbell rang again. My friend answered and there stood a man about 60 years old. "I need to see Dumitru Duduman. I want to talk to him."

My friend didn't respond, but the man came in anyway. I stepped forward and introduced myself. "I am Dumitru Duduman."

"Come with me into another room so we can talk." I followed him.

"My name is Constantine, and I am the Chief Commander of the Romanian Secret Police in Constanta. I have received a lot of complaints about you from Christians in Constanta. I decided to follow you and see what is going on. I came with you in the same train, and finally I found you here."

When he said these words, chills tingled in my spine. But he didn't give me much time for reflection. "Mr. Duduman," he continued, "don't be afraid. I will do no evil to you. Before I left town, I mentioned to my mother that the man I was about to follow was a Pentecostal Christian. 'What is his name?' she asked me. 'Duduman,' I told her. When she heard your name, she looked in my eyes and said, 'Do not dare, beloved son, to do anything evil to this man! He is a man of God. If you try to fight against him, God will punish you'."

I looked up at Constantine, and saw that there were tears in his eyes. "As long as I am the Chief Commander of the Secret Police in Constanta, you can visit the Christians there and nothing will happen to you. But there's one thing I want to ask of you... please, sir." He paused searching for words. "I have two more years until I retire. Please pray for me, that the Lord will have mercy on me. I want to turn to Him and find Him."

"Of course I will pray for you! God wants you to know Him!"

He left, and I shared this exciting story with the two other Christians who were visiting my friend's home. Later, as I listened to their continuing conversation, I heard them talking about Bibles. "Can you give me a Bible, too?" I asked.

"Yes, Brother Duduman, we can give you not just one,

but many!"

I was extremely curious as to how they obtained these Bibles, but didn't feel it was wise to ask right then.

The next day, when I got ready to go home, my host gave me a number of Bibles. "Brother Dumitru," he told me, "the Lord has prepared these Bibles for you. If you will be a secret courier, devoted to the Lord for His ministry, in the future you will receive more of these. You can take them to the Northern part of Moldavia where the lack of Bibles is so great. This will bring great joy to the believers."

All the way home from Bucharest, I was gripped with joy! I felt as if I had a suitcase full of diamonds. I worried a little too, because I was not sure just how God would enable me to give these Bibles to Christians without my being discovered by the Secret Police.

"How will I do it?" I repeatedly asked myself. Finally I determined that I would simply fast and pray. The Lord would tell me who should receive the Bibles.

In the days to come I gave those Bibles away, one by one, to sincere Christians who truly loved the Lord, and had no other resources. I was deeply moved in my spirit. For right before my eyes, I could see the beginning of the ministry the messenger from God had promised me!

"Lord!" I praised Him wholeheartedly. "You are wonderful! Not one of Your words remains unfulfilled!"

Before long, my wife and I were traveling back and forth, our suitcases bulging with Bibles. Of course it was a risk, but the Holy Spirit continually warned us of danger. Nothing happened to us. But, no matter how many Bibles we brought from Bucharest to Moldavia, it wasn't enough. Soon I located another source of Bibles, and we were able to deliver even more.

Throughout this time, many people were coming to the Lord... people I encountered in my travels. And the Lord continued to protect me from detection by the authorities. His hand was clearly upon me.

The work with the Bibles in this manner began in 1959. Time after time God would direct His people so healings could take place.

One night I had a vision. A messenger from God told me, "On the 3rd of February, you are to go to the town of Ilea. When you get off the train, there will be a man in a small car waiting for you. He will take you to some Christians. Don't worry that you have never been there before, because I will take care of you. I will write the license plate number on your right hand." He asked for my hand and put the number under the skin of my right hand. *(It was visible for a long time after the incident.)*

"Be sure this number matches the license plate number on the car," he instructed.

On the 3rd of February, I left on the train in the midst of a terrible snowstorm. I checked my hand to reassure myself that the numbers and letters of the license plate were still readable. The wind was howling when I got off the train. By now, it was terribly dark, and stinging snow blinded my eyes. I began to look around for the car that I'd been told about. Then I saw it! ...a Romanian Dacia - and the only vehicle in sight! As I approached the vehicle from the back, I studied the plate number. It matched the one on my hand. A man wearing a sheepskin coat was sleeping at the wheel. I approached the car and said, "Peace of God be with you Brother," startling him from his sleep. "Who are you waiting for?" I asked.

"I don't know," he replied. "But, about an hour ago a man dressed in white clothing came to me, woke me up and said, 'Go to the train station and pick up a man that is coming there. He's been sent by the Lord. Pick him up and take him where he needs to go'." I then showed him the number on my right hand. He was overjoyed and his faith was mightily increased.

Neither of us knew exactly what to do next. Then I saw a man sitting on the hood of the car, dressed as a policeman, with a sword in his hand. He began to direct the way. I told Brother Iordanel that we had another passenger... the angel of the Lord. Every time we were to turn, he would direct with the sword. We followed the angel's directions, then suddenly he held the sword with the tip pointing straight up. I asked Brother Iordanel what that could mean. "That is a sign to stop," he said.

We soon realized that we had been led by the Lord to a nearby village called Cimpuri Surduc. Just as we stopped the car, I saw a man running toward us; his hands in the air. As he approached the car, we could hear him saying, "Glory to God in the Highest, peace on earth, good will to men."

"My name is Jean Zenovi," he said. "I am the pastor in this town."

"The angel of God woke me from a deep sleep and sent me here, telling me that I needed to meet you. He will lead us to a place where he's going to do something wonderful."

Again, we didn't know where we were going, but the policeman on the hood of the car continued to direct us onward. Even though the snow was deep and made traveling difficult, we had no trouble. With the pastor along, we went on to another village. There we found a group of believers who had been fasting and praying for 40 days. They were deeply burdened for a young woman of nineteen years who was very ill. During their prayers, the Holy Spirit had promised them He would send someone with a gift of healing, who would pray for this girl. "We are so happy to have you here," they told us. "We praise God for His faithfulness!" I told them, "We are all just humans and have no power if God is not with us, but, if we pray and believe, we have what we ask."

Soon the young woman, Lydia, was healed by the Lord. She had been suffering from a huge goiter on her neck. She requested prayer. The first time we prayed, the goiter exploded with a loud sound. At the same time, in a vision from God, I saw a snake come out of the goiter. When we finished praying, I looked at her. The exploded skin was still hanging from her neck. We prayed a second time, and when I looked, the excess skin had dried up. A THIRD time, we prayed. When I looked again, the excess skin had fallen off and her neck looked completely normal. Her illness had been so severe that, when the others in the community saw her healing, they believed God could heal them too. It was a powerful thing to see Him moving so lovingly among the people there. God confirms His word to increase our faith.

Lydia told me she had a dream in which she saw me, so she believed she would be healed. She then told me her parents were not christians. Her father was the driver of a Secret Police car. He had told her, if God would heal her, he would sell his car, give half of the money to the poor, and give his life to the Lord.

But instead of fulfilling his commitment to God, he was angry with me because God had healed his daughter. He reported me to the Secret Police. Lidia called me and warned me against returning to Lipova, because the Secret Police were looking for me there.

(Many years later, while in Constanta, her father came to me and introduced himself. He told me he had not keep his promise to God. A few years later, he saw a goiter beginning to grow again on Lydia's neck. He immediately sold the car, gave half of the money to the poor, and gave his life to God. The goiter growth stopped, being about the

size of a cherry. Apologizing to me for what he had tried to do to me, he also said the little "cherry" on his daughter's neck was a sign for him to stay faithful to God.)

After praying with the Brothers in Lipova about four hours, Brother Iordanel said, "Let's go to Rosia, Arad. Feeling that to be direction from the Lord, we agreed. It was about a one hour drive. The only address we had was of the church. We thought if we went there, we would find someone to direct us to the pastor's home. It was not a regular meeting day, but when we arrived we heard voices in the church. Inside, we found 14 pastors in prayer. They said, "We were waiting for you. God told us you were coming, and we were to anoint you with oil."

I rejoiced in my spirit. "If the Lord wants me to be anointed, His will be done!"

The pastors took oil and anointed me with it. They laid their hands on my head and prayed for me. I felt even more power, strength and courage from God than ever before. From that moment on, I sensed that it would be my responsibility to continue in God's work in a mightier way than ever; never again shirking the duties that God would give me to do.

When we left, we decided to take the pastor of the Cimpuri Surduc church home. On the way there, the pastor invited me to stay overnight and come to the morning service.

After I finished preaching, I asked for those who needed healing to come forward. Many came forward, but one man called out, "I do! I do, God!"

As he came forward, I saw he was humped over. "What happened to you?" I asked.

He told me that when he became a Christian, his son-in-law, a Secret Policeman, beat him until he broke his back.

"Do you believe God is healing you?"

44

"Yes, God." he cried out, not speaking to me.

"If so, why don't you just straighten up, then?"

As soon as I had spoken, he stood up straight and ran out the door, praising God.

When he returned, he said, "I am not going to ride the 20 kilometers home, I am going to walk!!" And he did.

I later learned - when his family saw what God had done - they turned to God, also.

I continued my efforts, transporting Bibles to needy believers. Again and again I saw the eyes of the police turned away from me. My suitcases were stuffed with Bibles, and yet they seemed blinded to the fact that I was carrying the Word of God with me.

One night I was walking from the train station at Bucecea. It was 12 midnight, and I had heavy luggage filled with Bibles and other Christian literature. I was moving very slowly and painfully because of the heavy weight I carried. I must have been about three kilometers from my village when suddenly an enormous wolf charged out of the woods, rushing straight toward me.

At the sight of the ferocious beast, my legs seemed to freeze in their tracks. I was paralyzed with terror. The wolf got within about two feet of me, it's jaws dripping as it stopped to look me over.

"Dear Jesus!" I cried out, "You know I'm here because I'm trying to serve You. This luggage I carry is full of Bibles. Will You allow this wolf to kill me? No! I don't believe You will do that! I know that You are with me and Your hand is upon me! Please... help me get back to my family!"

Once these words had left my lips, I was somehow able to move my legs again. I started to go slowly and the wolf followed me at the same pace. He circled me, around and around, as I continued my unbearably slow progress.

Finally after what seemed like an eternity, I could see

the first dwelling of my village. When at last I reached the clearing, the wolf howled a terrible howl and abruptly turned and trotted back into the forest.

I fell on my knees, hot tears pouring down my face. "Thank you, God! You've delivered me again from grave danger."

During this time one of the pastors in Constanta died. His wife was so devastated by his passing that she grew ill. Her husband had been just 56 years old, and she seemed unable to cope with her loss. As the months passed, she developed violent headaches and seemed to be crying all the time. A year went by, and her condition worsened.

One day I received a telegram from her. "I will be coming to your home in the next few days. Please wait for me." Three days later she arrived with her son. "Will you pray for me to receive healing, Brother Dumitru?" She looked at me with pleading in her weary eyes.

It was very hard to pray in my home because the police were always around. But we decided to fast and pray that God would have mercy on her. We began a worship service with one song, then a Christian Brother began to pray very loudly. While he was praying I heard a noise outside. The dog started barking. I quietly walked out to the front of the house where the corn was tall. Hiding behind it, I peered around the corner to see who was there. As I looked out into the street, I saw a police car.

Three officers were inside the car listening. Fear immobilized me, because I could clearly hear the singing. I knew very well that the policeman could hear it, too. "There's no way out this time," I thought to myself. "They've caught me."

Next, I expected them to enter the gate. But listening carefully, I heard one of them speak. "You know, we have no brains. Those people are asleep and here we sit listening at their gate."

With that, they drove away.

When I saw them leaving, I felt like jumping up and down with joy. "Indeed, the angel of the Lord has been at my house protecting us!" I told the others. "Beloved brethren, we can praise God without being afraid... the Lord has deafened the ears of the authorities, and they cannot hear our praises!"

"Hallelujah," they all cried. "And in the same way, Sister Stela will be healed by the Lord tonight."

We all started to sing another song, and the power of the Holy Spirit came upon us. Anointing Stela with oil, we prayed for her. As we were praying, I saw a rat come out of her head. The rat started to attack young Mike Boldea, my oldest grandson. He was five years old at that time. When the rat got close to him he yelled, "Blood of Jesus!", and hid behind me. The rat immediately turned to the door and left.

"Sister Stela, did you feel the healing?" I asked

"Yes, Brother! I know the Lord has healed me!"

And so He had... her illness never returned. The Lord was using me to do a healing work among His people. Once again He was keeping His promises to me!

After God had done His work, I walked the Brothers out, then took the pail and went to fetch water. On my way to the well, I saw a soldier in full battle gear. He saluted me and sharply asked, "Going to get water?"

"Yes", I said. But my mind at the time did not find this awkward.

On my way back the soldier said, "Did you get the water?"

"Yes..." I stepped inside and suddenly my mind began to react. I told my family what I had seen. We felt a presence as I told them. Like little children, we all ran out,

47

looked around and examined the ground for signs - but nothing was found! We went back in and had a time of prayer. Then we went to bed. I did not even begin to doze yoff before the soldier appeared again; this time, above my grandson's head, who was sleeping in the room with me. "Who are you?" I asked.

He said, "I am an angel of God; the protector of your home."

After a long conversation, the angel left. Getting up I told my family what had happened.

He showed me His love once again. Not long after that I took another trip around the country, and as always stopped in Constanta. While there, I was asked by Brother Austecioae to visit the very leper colony to which Brother Andrei was almost sent. "I am terrified that we will never see our families again!" I told him.

Brother Austecioae responded, "What kind of a prophet are you? I will expose you to the people, that you have no faith! God will protect us, because there are Christians there who have sent for us. So rebuke the devil!"

As we rode along, again and again I heard the voice of the enemy saying, "You will never come back!"

At last we arrived. We had to leave the car outside the tall gates which were intended to keep visitors away. "WARNING: DO NOT ENTER!" a grim sign read, "YOU MAY CONTRACT LEPROSY IF YOU GO FURTHER!" Before we entered, officials required us to take blood tests. We signed affidavits stating that if the disease was found in our bloodstreams after the visit, we would have to stay.

"You'll never come out," The officers said. "Even the doctors get it." It took us a half day to get in. The doctors were surprised that we wanted to go in, but we assured them we were not going in alone. We stood on the promises in **Mark**: *"When they drink deadly poison it* *will not hurt them at all; they will place their hands on the sick people, and they will get well.*" Once inside, Brother Arseni Zurgiv, the godly man who ministered there, was so grateful that we had come. It was a place that I will never in my life forget. While I visited his home, this weary, faithful man of God began to tell me about his illness and the families he cared for. "Come with me. I need to visit some sick people." Then he told me how for many years he had suffered pain, "...until I trusted God with all my heart, and my sickness stopped progressing," he said.

I hope that I never again see people in the midst of such suffering!

"Lord," I prayed silently, "How can they endure so much?" The lepers were so undernourished that I could see every one of their ribs. The dreadful disease had disfigured them grotesquely. Some had no eyes; others - no cheeks, no ears, no hands. Some had even lost their legs.

After visiting the pathetically afflicted people that he cared for so lovingly, Pastor Arseni took me to the cemetery. He pointed to the resting places of a number of Christians. One of them was a man named Dr. Florin.

"He was a Christian doctor," Arseni explained, "and after finishing college at the age of 24, he came here of his own choice. His only desire was to save lives. Before long he contracted leprosy himself, and eventually it took his life. Although he died - because of his efforts, medicines were discovered that greatly help with this disease."

I began to cry. "Lord," I prayed in my heart, "would I ever be willing to give my life for a single Brother or Sister?" At that moment I didn't know the answer.

We returned to Pastor Iorge's "House of Prayer" which was located inside the Leper colony's gates. It was a good sized building, and was very well cared for. "Who built this place for you?" I asked him.

"Well, the ones with hands helped the ones without hands, and the ones with legs helped those that had no legs. It was very hard, but thank God the place is finished, and it gives us such joy to worship here! And you know, more than that, we are praying for you... the well ones. Our prayer is that God will keep you away from sin."

My mind was still spinning, trying to absorb his words, when the Christians began to gather. After the pastor made a sign with his hand, everyone began to sing. At the end of the service Pastor Arseni said, "I have Brothers and Sisters here that want to allow God to come into their hearts. And we have nobody to baptize them in water... I cannot with just one hand! If you would do this, Brother Dumitru, this would leave a joy and remembrance with us for the rest of our lives."

I did just as he asked, going into the woods to a river where eight new believers in Jesus followed their Lord in the waters of baptism.

Finally the day came for us to leave. We spent four days in the colony with them, then it took two more days to be checked and tested before we could go home. Once they were sure we were not infected they let us go. On our return visits they never stopped us; just let us pass.

We waved goodbye to our friends behind the big gates, which closed slowly behind us. I can still see them looking after us and hear their voices fading behind us.

"Lord," I prayed as we drove back to Constanta, "I'm healthy and free. I can return home to my wife, child and house. Sometimes I forget to praise You as I should. But those poor people are forever separated from their loved ones, and they are suffering incredible physical pain as well as emotional hurts. Yet they are praising You, Almighty God, and they are doing it with all their hearts!"

I had taken a step of faith, having such close contact

with leprosy's victims. But, of course, it never touched me at all. I even took home honey gathered by the lepers from their bee colonies, and my family and I shared it. After the honey was gone I told my wife and my daughter where it was from. At first Maria and Virginia were horrified that they had eaten honey from such a place. They began to scratch, their imaginations running wild! But, of course, they had no leprosy. God had protected us all.

I carried my story into the midst of the Constanta Baptist Church. I told them about the lepers we had met, and how their lives were filled with love for the Lord. The believers there wept and prayed for those less fortunate Brothers and Sisters. During this time of prayer, many of them started speaking in languages they had never learned. Clearly, God was continuing to do a mighty work there among the Baptists.

In the hours that followed my departure from Constanta, my travels sent me on a dizzying number of trains. When I had been in one city for about four hours, I got on another train, then changed twice more. When I finally got to Timisoara, I noticed I was being followed. I'd thought so earlier in the day and now there was my companion again.

I stayed in Timisoara four days so I could go to church there. I was invited to stay with a Christian Hungarian family. I was so glad to be with them. On Sunday we all went to church.

The pastor of this Pentecostal fellowship was a man who was obviously filled with the Holy Spirit of God. Once again I found myself used by God, for many were healed, baptized and filled with the Holy Spirit at that church.

When my four days ended, I took the train back to Constanta, looking for the policeman who had been following me along the way, I couldn't find him anywhere.

"I believe, at least here in Constanta, he will leave me. He won't follow me - I don't think..." Still, I wasn't quite sure.

I arrived at a Christian Brother's home, and when he saw me he began to rejoice. "How quickly you received our telegram!"

"What telegram?" I asked, puzzled at his words.

"I sent you a telegram asking you to come to us."

"I didn't receive any telegram, I've been away from home for nine days. It was the Holy Spirit that told me to come! Why did you want me here?"

"Well..." the man hesitated. "Of course we wanted to rejoice with you!"

"Of course, but..." I wondered just what he was getting at.

"You see, Brother Dumitru, the Baptists have excluded us from their church, so we want to start our own church."

My heart sank. I knew the story all too well. The battle for Romania wasn't between the Communists and the church. It was really between Satan and the Holy Spirit of God.

I remember so well, with much love, the Brethren who worked so faithfully with me in Romania. Some of them are now living in the United States. Some of these used their cars to bring the Bibles from sources near the borders where the missionaries would store them so they would not be caught. Then we would pick them up and take them wherever - even into Russia.

Chapter Four

WHO CAN BE AGAINST US?

Tired after a train trip of over twelve hours, I stopped at sister Marcica's house in Timisoara, for a prayer meeting. A prophetic word was given to me: "Listen, you who have arrived today. I have a work of great importance to do with you. Be prepared, for in a short time I will send a servant of mine to invite you somewhere. Go without fear or hesitation."

The prophecy was not yet over when Brother Nelu Neaga came through the door. When he saw me, his face shone with joy. "You know something? God works in ways which are hard for us to comprehend. I have been trying to reach you for a long time, and when I didn't even expect it, I have found you. Come with me to Almasu Mare tomorrow." Not having any other plans, and knowing what God had told me, I agreed. Midnight had just passed. I got back on the train which I had just gotten off. There was no place to sit, so I stood for almost 5 hours, even though tired.

It was not easy. But I knew I was obeying God, so I did it with joy. We finally arrived in Balk, but the bus that we were supposed to take had just left. We had to walk another hour and a half.

53

At 7:10 a.m. we got to the church of Almasu Mare. The church was already full, 2 hours before it was even scheduled to begin. I realized this was a special service. Exhausted, I entered the church and sat on the last bench near the coat rack. I took my coat off and covered myself with it, thinking I could take a little nap before church started.

I did not even have time to fall asleep because suddenly I heard a powerful "Hallelujah!! This is what the Lord sayeth: My servant, through which I want to fulfill my plan, is here." Then someone said, "Who was sent of the Lord? Come up." No one came up. Again the person said, "Then Brothers, let us pray that God will show us who he is." The prayers of the Brothers went up like thunder.

Then the same man who had spoken, began to look on every row of benches, looking at every Brother's face. I was on my knees, truly not thinking about anything. The man came to the right of me. "You there! Look at me!" He spoke to the Brothers, "Brothers, he is the one that God has shown me," speaking of me. He turned back to me, "Come with me." When I got off my knees to go to the pulpit, everyone exploded in prayer with a new burst of energy. Not knowing what was going on, I got behind the pulpit and waited for the prayer to end so that I would know what was to happen. The prayer ended two and a half hours later. Never in my life had I seen such a powerful prayer.

The building shook, and on the roof was a flame about two meters high. Non-christians came with buckets of water to put out the fire. This was not a fire which man could extinguish.

About halfway through the prayer I saw the door open, and a young lady about twenty years old walked in. She got on her knees, but did not say a word. Suddenly, the power of God took her off the floor. She floated to the front before the pulpit. There she was gently put down.

"Lord, I thank You for healing me," she said. For the first time in her life, the voice of this young lady was heard - and she was thanking God! The congregation was so excited they exploded into instant prayer for more than an hour! When the prayer subsided, the pastor came to me with tears in his eyes and said, "She is my daughter and she was born mute. We fasted and prayed for 40 days for her healing. We even built a house for a poor family in our town, during the 40 days. The Lord has answered our prayers." Then they called me forward to speak. After about 10 minutes of preaching, I heard a voice in my ear, "Run! The police are coming for you!"

I did not hesitate. I told Brother Neaga and we left the church through the back door. We were taken to the Oradea train station by car. The train began to slowly move only a few seconds after we got on. Looking back, I saw those who had been chasing me. Waving at them, I rejoiced for the victory in the Lord.

For about two more weeks, I continued to travel, doing God's work. Then I returned home.

A short time later, I headed for Deva, taking Brother Pavel with me.

We traveled about 9-10 hours by train. Arriving at the local pastor's home, his wife greeted us. "Welcome!", she said.

"Is your husband home?" I asked.

"No, my husband is working in the pasture and will be out there for some time. Would you like to come with me?"

"Where are you going?" I was very tired from the train journey, but curious about her mission.

"Right now I'm preparing to visit a woman who has

cancer. It would be good if you would come with me so you can give her a word of comfort. She is so ill, we are expecting her to die any time."

"Of course I'll go with you!" I answered. We left together immediately to visit the woman whose name was Lidia Moga.

I had never met her before, and had never in my life seen anyone more visibly ill. Lidia was lying in her bed - so thin that there was really nothing left of her but skin and bones. She had not been moved off that bed for six consecutive months.

Lidia had six young children and lived in obvious poverty. Her husband worked far away and was only able to return home on the weekends. The house was filthy. The little children were far too small to help with the work. Now and then a Christian Sister would come and clean. The sight and stench of the place were appalling. Anna, the pastor's wife, asked me to wait outside until she tidied up the place a bit.

When I entered and approached Lidia's bed, I said, "Peace of the Lord to you, dear Sister."

"Same to you," she murmured. I could hardly hear her voice.

"Sister, has anybody prayed for you?"

"Yes, they have," she answered very weakly. "Many times they have anointed me and prayed for me."

All at once the Lord showed me that she was filled with doubts. "Well, what do you say? If I pray for you, do you believe you will get well?"

"No," she quickly responded. "No, I don't believe."

"God!" I prayed silently in my heart. "God, can't You give a gift of healing to a mother of six children? Hallelujah! I know You can!"

Suddenly I felt surge of spiritual power. "If you don't

believe," I burst out, "I'll believe in your place! In Jesus name I command you to get out of bed!"

"Thank you Lord, for healing me!" she cried.

When I finished my prayer I looked around. Sister Lidia was not in the bed anymore! Instead she was on her knees by the door thanking God for healing her. Gone was her feeble voice. She was yelling at the top of her lungs, "Thank You God! Thank You God!"

She told me that when I commanded her to get out of bed, the power of God lifted her from the bed and set her on the floor on her knees.

This miracle was one more sign of God's fulfilling His promise to use me.

That evening, at the local church, the Pastor suggested they pray for Sister Lidia, not knowing what had happened earlier. As they finished praying for her, she entered the church and began thanking God for healing her. Many people in need of healing were healed, and those who asked for the Baptism of the Holy Spirit received.

Although she had a hysterectomy before the healing, she gave birth to two more children, surprising her doctor and those who knew of her surgery.

The next morning I left for Bucharest to see Brother Caraiman. When I arrived, he invited me to a prayer meeting. As we headed toward the meeting I suddenly had a vision. A soldier appeared in front of the car and stopped us with his rifle. I was terrified!

"Lord, what does this vision mean?" I silently asked Him. I described to the men what I had just seen. They shook their heads, uncertain as to what the interpretation might be.

The vision frightened me because when it happened I had a strong impression that some kind of danger was imminent. I just couldn't imagine what it would be.

The three of us arrived at the prayer meeting which was taking place in secret in a room under a house. I got on my knees there and started to pray. All at once the Holy Spirit showed me that there was an undercover policeman in our midst. The Lord told me, "He has been coming here for six months and telling his supervisor all about the meetings."

During the same prayer the Holy Spirit spoke through me to a particular man who appeared to be worshipping with the rest of us. "Listen! You are only pretending to be a Christian. You are not one. Today I will stop your work because you are the enemy of the Lord Jesus Christ!"

I didn't even have time to get up from my knees when the tall man, to whom I had been speaking, lunged toward me and thrust a gun into my chest. Instantly, Brother Tache, who stood beside me, reacted. He jumped up, grabbed the gun and disarmed the under cover officer. "You can't harm the man of God!" he shouted.

When the policeman realized that he had no weapon, he began to talk. "My name is Eugene. For six months I have been coming here as if I were a good Christian. In fact, I wasn't one at all. I was a betrayer of you all. I am a lieutenant in the Secret Service. My mission is to do evil. I had told myself there is no God, so all of this is a lie, but tonight I realize that God <u>does</u> exist."

"Hallelujah!" someone shouted, breaking the icy silence that had chilled the room.

"Yes, God <u>does</u> exist, and He has brought to light the evil thing that I have been doing. Will you forgive me? Please pray for me that God will not punish me for the things I've done."

"God is your judge, not us," I told him.

He wasn't finished with what he had to say and interrupted me. "Today I have seen there is a supernatural power that comes directly from God. This power is higher than any power. I can see that He is your Light and your Leader. He is wiser than anybody else. You are the servant of a living God! I repent," the lieutenant concluded, his face bathed with tears, "from all my evil!"

Lieutenant Eugene gave up his job, his money, his honors and everything else that day. He went on to serve the Lord with all his heart. We all rejoiced with this man. And we thanked the Lord for doing such a mighty work of grace in his heart. Later we learned that he had dedicated his life to the service of God and had received the Holy Spirit into his life.

The next day, loaded down with a few suitcases of Bibles, I headed for Suceava from Bucharest. As usual I was traveling at night, because the connections were better. Almost ten hours had passed since I had left. Suddenly a voice woke me up. "Get up and get off. You're in Veresti." Before realizing what was going on I took my luggage and got off. As I stepped off, the train left. There I was in the middle of a big field, without even a dim light to guide my path. I then realized the train had stopped for a sign. Troubled, I began to walk. Not knowing how much time had lapsed, I pressed on and, finally, I began to see the dim lights of the train station. Getting closer, I began to rub my eyes not believing what I was seeing before me. The train I had been on was almost destroyed, and the car that I had been in was nowhere to be seen.

As I aproached, people saw me and began to ask,"Where did you come from?" "Are you a survivor from the crash?"

This was yet another example of the Lord's protection over His people as well as His saving grace. In our prayer meetings we frequently saw the police either diverted or blinded to our existence. This was also the case when we delivered Bibles.

Many, many times when the police stopped us, God did not allow them to take us to prison. Later in my life, He would allow me to suffer greatly at the hands of the Communists, but during most of my years as a smuggler, He kept me miraculously safe.

God had a way of closing the eyes of the authorities. They simply could not see the Bibles we carried with us. We were often full of fearful emotions, but in spite of our weakness, the Lord's hand was with us.

No matter how difficult life became, it always strengthened me when I remembered that Jesus had suffered so much more than I had. He suffered to the end without defending Himself.

Despite the obstacles, the persecutions, the tortures - as we continued our efforts, Bibles were transported in greater and greater quantities. No matter what price was paid in human suffering, the Word of God was able to reach a growing number of people.

God gave wisdom even in our secular work for the government. Once I came upon an Orthodox priest from a nearby village, who was always harassing the protestants. He was carrying home an illegal catch of fish! I could have put him in jail for it, but I chose to take the fish from him and tell him to back off from giving the Christians problems. "If I catch you again like this, I will put you in jail!" I warned him. He gladly went his way and became very peaceable. I never caught him with illegal fish again!

Sometimes, when times were difficult, and my heart grew heavy with the struggle, I remembered that Jesus will one day return in the clouds. I knew I would one day meet Him. What would He say to me? "Well done, Dumitru, you are a good and faithful servant?" Oh, how I prayed that He would keep me, so those would be the words reaching my ears upon His return. I knew there would be everlasting joy, then. Our problems, our struggles, our tears, would exist no more.

Despite all their difficulties, one thing I miss about being among Romania's Christians is that they find such joy in simple things. They take great pleasure in simply visiting each other, traveling from city to city, from village to village. They love to gather together just to rejoice in the Lord. But even seemingly harmless social habits are frowned upon by the Communists. Many times the Secret Police detained Christians and arrested them. They would be fined several months pay for breaking the simplest of rules.

Once Maria and I organized a "Love feast" in our village. Christians from many other areas were invited to join us. My wife and I looked forward to this unique occasion for weeks. We had invited everyone to gather at our home for prayer. A hundred or more people would be there.

The pastor of the Orthodox church in our village hated the Pentecostals. He was very prejudiced against us, and when he heard about our meeting, he notified the authorities. While we were all eating at my home, there was a knock on the door.

"Good afternoon, Duduman." A slight smirk twisted the caller's mouth.

"Good afternoon." I recognized the man at the door as the captain of the Secret Police in my village. I fought off the feelings of fear that rippled through me. Such encounters were happening with greater frequency. Was this the beginning of the end of my ministry?

"When you finish eating, come to the police station."

"All right..." I began to close the door.

"Have you understood me?"

"Yes, I understand."

I shut the door and returned to the warm, lively crowd.

Everyone was feasting, laughing and having a wonderful time. I waited until the dinner was over, then told the people what had happened. The Secret Service wanted to talk to me. We all fell on our knees together in prayer. As we sought the face of God, asking for His wisdom and encouragement the word of the Holy Spirit came through the lips of one Brother.

"Do not be afraid. I am with you. No evil will happen to any of you. Your enemies who want to do evil to you will be defeated. I will come against them and punish them."

As we concluded our time of prayer, we vaguely noticed the sound of sirens in the roadway just outside.

Across the street from my house was the home of the priest. Next to his home was the police station. It was a busy area, and on that particular Sunday there were a lot of people milling around outside, people who obviously had been drinking more than their share of alcohol.

As I started to head for the police station I realized that there was a great deal of activity going on. What had happened?

For a moment or two I looked around, trying to see what was going on around me. I almost forgot my own problems.

"What happened?" I asked a bystander.

"Well, you see, some drunks started a fight. A captain and four police officers tried to stop them and the people in the fight were so wild that they beat the policemen into unconsciousness."

I quickly realized that the very captain who had been at my door was the one injured in the fight.

"It was so bad," the woman went on, "that all five police officers had to be taken to the emergency room."

"I, the Lord will come against your enemies and punish them..." the Lord had promised in our prayer meeting. He had done just as He said. But, He wasn't finished yet!

Just as I was absorbing all this, the ambulance screamed past us. A car screeched up and the occupants scrambled out quickly. Obviously they had come from the scene of another accident.

"Now who is being taken to the hospital?"

"It's the priest from the Orthodox church, Father Neron."

"What happened to him?" I asked, knowing very well that he was the informer who had reported our prayer and fellowship time to the Secret Service.

An older man shook his head. "Oh, he went out to feed his animals and milk his cow. Something scared the horse and as he was milking the cow, the horse kicked him and broke three of his ribs."

When I heard this, I turned around and went home. "Praise the name of the Lord," I said, when I reunited myself with all my guests, who had been praying in my absence. I told the brethren what had happened.

Later on I went back to the police department. When I got there I went directly to the Chief of Police.

"I was told by the Captain to come and see you," I informed him. "Well, Dumitru, you came for nothing. Those who wanted to arrest you have gotten into problems of their own. Your God, the one you all pray to and trust so much, has delivered you from the hands of your enemies."

I looked at the man in disbelief. He continued to speak, smiling a little at my amazement.

"You're free to go home. I have received direct orders from the Captain. He said, 'Do no evil to Dumitru or something worse will happen to you.'"

Again and again, our Lord kept His spoken Word. Again He had delivered His faithful servants. The days were coming when more suffering would descend upon my house. But for the time, God was choosing to keep me and my loved ones from the hand of the destroyer.

Not long after, two women, Marica and her sister, Magdalena came to our home. As always, when they first came in, we prayed. God showed me that Marica had uterine cancer, and had been hemorrhaging for six years without stopping!

When I had confirmed this with Marica, we gathered our prayer group to pray for her. I anointed her with oil, and we prayed. When we stopped praying, her hemorrhaging stopped! She has been completely whole ever since! Praise God!

I always wanted to obey God's direction in my life, but one time I let myself be swayed.

One year about a week before Christmas, I received a telegram from the city of Cimpina. It said, "Come quick! My mother is dying! - Carmen"

When I told Maria she responded, "Oh, no! You're not going again! You just got <u>back</u> from a tour. This time I want you to stay home!" I didn't feel good about it, but she convinced me to stay.

That evening, I went to my nephew's, home (Victor), who was an electrician. When I opened the door to step inside, there was an non-insulated wire hanging near my face. I reached out with my hand, to move it aside, saying, "What's this?" As I Grasped the wire, Victor unplugged the 220 Volt breaker. But it was too late! In the moment before the voltage stopped, my hand was burned to the bone!

It was so painful, I immediately went home, bandaged my hand and left for the Aron family prayer meeting in Dumbraveni without telling anyone.

When I arrived, I hid my hand so no one would know I had been burned. If God had a word for me, I wanted to be sure no one would be influenced. I asked everyone to

64

pray. While we were praying, a prophecy came forth. "Are you hurting? No, you are not hurting compared to the person who called you to come and pray for her. Go! If you do, I will heal your hand."

I went home and TOLD Maria I was going to pray for the mother. Maria said nothing, because she saw what was happening.

When I got on the train, the pain in my hand stopped. During the train ride to Anna's home, the open wound began to seal over.

When I arrived at Anna's home (Carmen's mother), she was so ill her entire family was grieving; expecting her to die. She had been in bed over three years. I anointed her with oil, and prayed for her. God instantly healed her.

I then began to preach to the family. They ALL became Christians; her two daughters, her son-in-law, and another couple from the neighborhood.

I stayed for two more days, praying with them and teaching them. (During this time, my hand continued to heal. By the time I arrived home, God had completely healed my hand.) I also helped them find a church to attend. Then I left for Bucharest.

After a few days with friends, I left for home, bringing their son, Teofil, with me for a one month visit.

On the train ride home, Between Fetesti and Baragan, the train collided with a bulldozer. There were about eight people in the coach I was riding, including a woman with a baby. She was sitting in front of me - facing. When we collided, the baby flew out of the woman's arms and landed in mine. The woman split her head on the window and the young man with me split his head on a mirror. Everyone in the coach was injured except the baby and me.

I know that no matter what happens around us, if God chooses to protect us, we will not be harmed!

MY FAMILY IN 1958

PREPARING A "LOVE FEAST"

Chapter Five

BIBLES FOR RUSSIA

By 1973, my precious little daughter had somehow become a bright-eyed, attractive young lady and several local young men were exhibiting some serious interest in her. Although she knew that any one of them would be proud and happy to be her husband, Virginia believed that the choice of a marriage partner was a decision only God could wisely make. I was proud to hear that she had committed the choice to Him.

The following year, Maria and I bought tickets to visit friends all around the country. Virginia was to go with us.

The Sunday before our departure, the Lord gave her an exciting prophecy through a godly friend. "Listen, young lady, you have said that you will let Me choose you a husband and that you will not choose him yourself. Now, on the trip that you are about to make you will meet the man of MY choice!"

At about that same time, a man in the church had a vision of a young, brown-haired man with a dimple on his right cheek. He saw that Virginia would meet him walking down a road, but would not know that he was the one God had chosen.

Two days before we were to leave, a Christian friend came to visit us. Virginia was not at home at the time, but the man persisted in telling us all about his nephew who was an intelligent, good looking and very nice young man. He also invited us to stay in his home and visit his family while we were on our trip. We agreed to do this.

We caught the train at the Faget Station, and were walking toward Bichigi when we encountered a young man walking in our direction. When Virginia saw him, she whispered excitedly to Maria, "If I could find a boy like that, I would marry him!"

We went on to the home that was our destination. Soon, after a warm greeting, we all sat down to eat. As we were enjoying a delicious meal, the host family's young nephew walked in through the door. It was Mike - the boy we had met on the road! Mike was the young man our friend had been telling us about during his visit to our home! When Virginia saw him and realized what she had said to her mother, she dropped her spoon.

We stayed there in Bichigi a couple of days, then we went on to another city.

While we were gone, Mike's family declared a fast for three days. They wanted God to let them know if Virginia was to be his wife. "If so, let the Dudumans come back to our house!" they prayed together. In a short time I was called to pray for a man in Deva who was gravely ill. He lived in a town close to Bichigi. To no one's surprise, while we were on our way, Virginia suddenly said, "Let's go back to Bichigi and visit those people again."

We did so, but there was no discussion of marriage. We soon left for Timisoara. After a few days of ministry, we departed for Constanta.

The people were excited to see us, again. On Sunday, during the service, a Brother leaned over to me and

68

whispered, "See that man behind you? He's a Secret Service man, who has been following you since you left Timisoara."

Soon I was called to preach, but knowing the Secret Service man was there for me, I was unable to speak. For 10-15 minutes I just stood still. Everyone thought I was receiving a vision from God. Finally, I felt a power come over me. I cried out, "Hallelujah! The power of God then fell on the entire church. A prophecy came forth, "You who came here with the burden for Me to heal you - I will surely heal you today!" A woman stood up and said she had cancer. She showed her stomach area, and we saw a cancerous infection eaten clear through to the surface. She said, "See this?! God is going to heal this!"

After prayer she again showed the same area. It appeared as though there had NEVER been ANY cancer!

Before we had started praying, a non-christian woman stood up and said, "I came here to be healed too. A man appeared in my hospital room this morning and told me to come here to be healed." This woman was on the verge of death. But when we prayed, God healed her, also. She gave her life to God that morning.

At the same time, a man possessed of the devil, fell to the floor near the Secret Service man, and began writhing and screaming. The Secret Service man stood up, covered his head with his hands and cried out, "Please tell Mr. Duduman not to harm me! Tell him not to pull my hair out!" He then turned and ran out the door, and never returned.

Though I could do nothing, I was thrilled that GOD was in charge of all.

From there we returned home. In just a few days Virginia received a letter from Mike, asking if he could come and visit, since he needed to call upon some Christians in our area. "Yes," she told him.

In March he arrived. Just before he had left home, he had a dream that he and Virginia were to be married. He had asked the Lord to confirm the dream in church. God gave him a prophecy that very morning in our fellowship telling him that the dream was indeed real. After the service he walked Virginia home and told her about his dream and its confirmation. "Will you marry me?"

"Yes," she said!

Fathers are fathers, and Mike might not have been the man I would have chosen for my daughter, but Maria would have none of my objections. "Nobody told YOU who to marry, and this is none of your business! Keep still!"

The beautiful wedding was May 5, 1974. It wasn't long after the two were married that he became involved in the work we all so fully shared. Mike has been a sharing, faithful member of our family ever since.

Bibles, Bibles, Bibles. The matter of their delivery continued to be the focus of my thoughts. Nothing could be more dangerous... it was an immense risk every time we took part in a smuggling mission, but God protected us. We were stopped many times. The police would check our cars and find nothing, even though they were filled with Bibles. Fear would pound in our hearts, but our joy was equally intense as we watched God faithfully protect us.

Both *Open Doors* and *Door of Hope* delivered Bibles near the border so it would be easier for us to get them. From there they were brought to my house, and we were able to transport them across the Russian border.

At first it was very hard to make contacts inside Russia, so we began to fast and pray about how to make the right "friends".

One night we were sleeping soundly when suddenly someone shook me by the shoulder and woke me up. At first I thought it was Maria, but she appeared to be asleep.

Was she teasing me, pretending to sleep? I raised one of her eyelids and said, "Maria, did you wake me up?"

She was angry with me saying, "NO! Let me go back to sleep! Why did you wake me up? You had a dream, then accused me of waking you up?".

I knelt down beside the bed and prayed. I returned to bed, but was unable to sleep. Then I felt a hand on my shoulder, and a voice said, "Wake up, Dumitru." This time I looked up and saw a man dressed in white shiny clothes.

"Do you want to take Bibles to Russia?"

"Yes!" I quickly replied.

He said, "Because you have asked, I came to help you." The man gave me an address in Radauti, a city not far from the Russian border, located beside the railroad line that runs into Russia. He said, "I will go before you. When you get there, a man will ask what you want. Tell him, 'I am sent by the same person who just visited you'."

I got up, dressed and went out. When I arrived in Radauti, I knocked on the door. A man opened the door, trembling with fright. "What do you want?" he asked.

"I am sent by the same person who just visited you," I said. "I want to send Bibles into Russia, and I want you to help me."

Trembling even more, the man invited me in. Soon he explained to me what we could do to get the Bibles across the border. He pointed to a key hanging on the wall, by the door. "Take it, bring the Bibles and store them in my basement. Then, here's what we'll do..." He went on to describe his plan:

When a boxcar load of furniture would come into the station, he would pull it off the line, saying the car had to be checked and the wheels adjusted for the Russian tracks, which differ in width from the tracks in Romania. The car would then be unloaded and the

71

furniture stored. While the furniture was in storage, with the help of several other men, some of whom would stand guard, we would take the Bibles from the basement and put them in the furniture, which would then be loaded back into the box cars. When the car was put back on the railroad line, it was on its way to Russia with no problem, whatsoever. Across the border, it would be unloaded and a Brother named Costiniuc would distribute the Bibles.

One blessing quickly became evident. When it came to smuggling Bibles into Russia, no difference was ever made with regard to the various denominations who wanted them. We gave to all of them with joy. Some nights we took Bibles to Dornesti to store them in a basement, where they would be transferred to train for shipment to Russia. When a load of furniture would come through about every two weeks, the car would be pulled off the main line and we would pass another load of Bibles into Russia. Other nights we took them to Stinca, where they would be delivered to Russia by car or on foot. Many times, when I would take Bibles from my home to store them, I would return to find the police checking my house.

Even though they could find nothing, they would still take me to the police station and keep me in jail for a day or two. There they made great sport of punishing me. My hand would be shoved into the door hinge, and the door slammed against my fingers. My face would be slapped and spit upon as they tried to force me to tell them who was helping me take Bibles across the Russian border. In spite of all this, God helped me not to reveal anything. I felt I would rather die than betray my Christian Brothers.

One example of the harassment was when my grandfather died. He was 115 years old and was the only Christian in his village. The Communists detained me and put me in jail so I could not attend his funeral. I cried and was angry, but nothing changed their minds.

Meanwhile, the volume of work was growing steadily. Soon it was so much we couldn't fit all the Bibles into our little cars. To our amazement we had to start using trucks and trailers.

I was contacted by more missionaries and missions with Bibles to donate. I always prayed and fasted, asking God whether to go or not to go. I wanted to work in His power, and not in my own. I believe it was because of this commitment that not one Bible got lost or fell into the hands of the police or Secret Police. The life of worry caused me to stay close to God, and He protected me with His strong hand. Even when we were being followed by the police, we never stopped getting together for prayer.

At one time there had been many Bibles among the church people. But the communist government did not allow them to keep the Bibles, so they confiscated them all! I was surprised one morning when I woke up to find a whole truckload of the confiscated Bibles dumped in my front yard. I told Maria, "We can't just leave them here!" So we picked them all up carefully checking each one for the name of the owner. We put them away out of sight and then I went on my bike or walked to return each book to its owner. I did this without anyone knowing. Sometimes I put them in the mailbox or left them on the doorstep so they would find them in the morning. It took me many nights to complete this project.

One day I received notice that I was to report to the police at Dorohoi. I was gripped with fear and went to the house of a Christian friend for prayer. The Holy Spirit came and spoke through him. "Listen, I have been with you always and have protected you every time. I will be with you this time also, and will save you. Don't be afraid. I will not let you down."

I went back home and got dressed. With tears in my eyes I said goodbye. I was very emotional because I knew all too well what this meant. I had been through similar encounters many times before. I took a bus from Hintesti, traveling two hours to Dorohoi. I prayed every mile of the way. I kept asking myself what they would do to me. I received no answer.

I went straight into the police station, and the officer in charge began interrogating me, promising me if I would answer him, everything would be much easier on me. After a little while, he saw he was getting nowhere, so he left. Soon his superior, a colonel, entered the room. He was an ugly, gangling man with a moustache. He glared at me, and began cursing God's name.

"Tell me," he snarled, "how can you afford to feed all of those Christians and nearly have a church in your house?"

"I feed my Brothers with God's help."

"What did you do with the Bibles that we left in your yard? Did you put them with the others that you have stored up?"

"God knows. I don't."

When he heard my words, he started cursing at me saying, "God again! I will get this God business out of your head once and for all! I'll show you!" He put his face right by mine, as close as he could get it, and he whispered hoarsely and angrily, "Come on. Tell me, how many missionaries are you dealing with?"

Seeing that I would not respond, he called in a superior officer who spat out the words, "Come with me! You will tell me everything. You'll even answer questions I don't ask!"

Guards roughly shoved me into a filthy jail cell. It was pitch dark. They slammed the door and left me there. For some time it was quiet. Then I heard another door open and close, but I saw nothing. Then I began to hear strange noises. Suddenly I felt something crawling up my legs! I grabbed at them, throwing them off. Rats! I continued grabbing frantically at them trying to throw them to the floor. They began to jump on my back - my head - all over me! I cried out to God, "God, are you going to let me die like this...?"

I didn't have time to finish my prayer when a bright light came into the room and a voice commanded me, "Dumitru look at me!"

I raised my eyes, but the light was so bright I couldn't look. He was clothed so brightly it blinded me. At the waist he had a shining belt. He had a huge flaming sword in his hand. Again he said, "Look at me! I am Gabriel - the Commander of God's army. God has heard your prayers." He went on to say, "I will put fear in the hearts of those who hate you. I will also cause them to set you free. Now close your eyes."

I closed my eyes, and after a few seconds he said, "Open your eyes, and look down." When I looked down, all the rats were dead! Gradually the light dimmed, and finally the angel was gone.

After a long time the silence made the guards curious. Suddenly the door burst open! The colonel looked in. When he saw all the dead rodents he began to scream, "You have killed all my children! Get out of here! Go home! All my children are dead!" He struck me in the head with his baton, had me beaten, and sent me home.

Soon we were back at work delivering the Bibles. We fasted and prayed and God sent more Bibles. He also closed the eyes of those that inspected the cars so they could go through undetected. It was a tremendous risk each time we moved our precious cargo, but God unfailingly protected us. Only true believers were chosen to take Bibles. We chose people who lived clean lives and served God continually. We all needed every bit of spiritual strength we could muster to help us face the hardships and constraints that might eventually occur.

Many times in Romania, pastors are paid by the government to inform on the activities of the believers - even to the extent that two men came to my house saying they were sick and wanted healing. They claimed they had heard about a Sister we had prayed for who was healed after being bed-ridden for four years. One claimed to have heart trouble; the other, stomach trouble. I was at a loss for words for an instant, then the Holy Spirit showed me they were government agents. I boldly told them, "You are not my Brothers. You are not sick, nor do you believe in God. Why do you pretend to be someone you are not?" Upon seeing they were discovered they took out their badges, arrested me and took me to Dorohoi. There they interrogated me, laughed at me, spit on me and told me if I didn't settle down and quit praying for sick people, they would put me in jail and I would never get out! I told them, "You decide if it is more important to listen to people or to God." The captain asked, "Isn't Duduta a pastor and Brother with you? How is it that he listens to us and even keeps us informed with the latest news of Christians?"

I answered, "He will answer to God for what he does." The colonel responded, "We'll see how you act to his face." He grabbed me and took me to another room where I could see Pastor Duduta through a glass.

"What do you say we do with Duduman?" asked the colonel.

"Sentence him to prison. He came to my church and prayed for sick people, a lot of times," was the response.

A door opened and I was shoved into the room with

Pastor Duduta. "Go shake hands with your "**Brother**" Duduta!"

"He is not my Brother. If he were, he would not betray the Christians." The colonel said, "He hates you because God uses you in all the churches."

I answered that. "I do not know what harm there is in praying for the sick and to have joy with your fellow brethren. I don't take any money from anyone nor do I trick anybody."

The colonel turned to Duduta. "Are you doing this and trying to put blame on those who are merely trying to keep their religion?"

"I needed the money because I have a big family."

The colonel began to slap and knock him around saying he was a thief and traitor, until Duduta cried that he would tell him everything. The colonel then dismissed me telling Pastor Duduta, "Duduta, the one who digs someone else's grave will himself fall into it." I later learned that they took Duduta's pastor's license from him and about two months later he died. (The God of Daniel still protects those who serve Him.)

And still there were more Bibles and more missionaries. They came from Germany, America, Holland. There were so many that the police were worried. They couldn't locate the source, nor could they keep up with the traffic of Bibles. There were simply too many Bibles. The harder they tried, the more God protected His people. We transported Bibles by train, bus, and trailers. Many of them were bound for Russia.

One of our best systems was to work through the mines. Mine trucks traveled back and forth between Romania and Russia every day. Every time we sent Bibles, a member of my family would go and check to see that they made it safely, taking clothes and money for those in need.

Usually this went to the families of the ones who had been put in prison because of the Lord's work.

One time, after we had sent a particularly large load of Bibles, I went personally to check that it had arrived at the given destination. I had a hard time getting a visa into Russia. Then, once I had finally crossed the border at Vadu Siret, I was called aside and questioned as to whether I had Bibles or religious books. First I was interrogated and searched at the Romanian check point, and then again at the Russian Check point. Fortunately I passed through both safely, taking with me some rubles for the Russian Brothers.

What a joy it was to take part in religious services being held in Cernauti, Russia. They were meeting inside a tent beside a destroyed church which the Communists had bulldozed down just a few days before. I thought to myself, "Nothing stops them from worshipping God... not rain, snow or the police." But while we were praying, one of them suddenly whispered, "Let's go! The police are coming!"

Soon eighteen police cars and four fire trucks pulled up. The fire hoses began dousing the tent with forceful streams of water while the police began beating everyone in sight... men, women and children! It was a heart breaking sight. My companion Constantin and I barely escaped to our hotel, and even in the relative safety of that place, we were up all night reliving the terror that we had seen.

In the Communist world, the police are often against the people. Discrimination is widespread, and no matter how much education a person has or what kind of work he does, if he does not belong to the Communist Party, he is not respected. He cannot get a good job, and he is unable to defend himself. Christian families are the neediest families of all.

One gloomy February night I was taking Bibles across

the border again. It was bitterly cold and blizzard conditions made traveling nearly impossible. We couldn't use the back roads so we had to travel the main highway where the police would be checking all suspicious vehicles. We covered about twenty-five kilometers without any problems. Then we realized that we were being followed.

At that very moment the angel of the Lord appeared to us and told us to turn right on a road that led into the forest. We didn't get far before our wheels were stuck in the snow. We couldn't move backwards or forwards. We were desperately afraid of being caught, so we got out and carefully hid the Bibles in the snow Then we waited a few hours. It grew colder with every passing minute. The hours seemed endless, and we were almost frozen.

"God," I cried out, "send someone to help us!"

The angel spoke to us again, saying, "Don't worry. I will send you help." With that he vanished.

Within moments we heard the voices of the border patrol guards. "What are you doing here?" they asked.

"We are not from this area. We're lost and snowbound."

"Good work, guys. You'd better come with us to the post so you don't freeze to death. We'll come back in the morning to get your car out of the ditch."

As we walked, my legs were so numb I couldn't feel them. But we were soon warming ourselves beside a fire, and were able to rest comfortably at the post until morning. Then we accompanied the guards and their bulldozer back to our snowbound car. I held my breath as the vehicle was dislodged from its snow bank, hoping the Bibles would not be revealed. They weren't!

After staying with a friend in Hlipiceni for two days we returned to get the Bibles. We searched everywhere for them, but every snow-covered mound looked like the next one. We began to pray together. A voice spoke to us both. "Look around where you see the light." Our eyes searched the snow, and all at once a little, glimmering light flickered across the way. We rushed over and started digging where it shone.

There were the Bibles! We frantically dug them out, loaded them into the car and headed for the border. As we rode along we heard a now-familiar voice. "Don't be afraid, for I am with you. Those guarding tonight will be sleeping. They won't hear or see you."

It was just as he promised. We made our way across the border, found some faithful Baptist Brothers and gave them the Bibles. Grateful, we returned home, praising God for the way he had given us the victory. Often we could cross the border where there was no check point. I would turn around and walk backward, so that it would appear that someone came from Russia into Romania and then when I returned it would appear they had come back from Romania in to Russia.

By April 1980 we had sent a lot of Bibles into Russia. I decided to go see what was going on with the Christians who had received them. When I got to Cernauti, the first message I heard was that the Costiniuc Christian men had been arrested and their families didn't have anything to eat. I couldn't get near them because they were heavily guarded, so I went back home wondering how I could help the families. I prayed to God to give the solution in the shortest time possible. I also shared the problem with my family. We decided that Virginia and Mike, along with some cousins, should go help these two families.

God worked out the details and soon my children were given passports and visas. Before they went, all of us fasted and prayed for God to protect them and guard the provisions they were taking with them.

They arrived at the border where all Romanian visitors were held to be checked. Those who had too much in their packages would have to pass an inspection. There were seven people ahead of them when the chief inspector approached Virginia. "Bring your packages and come with me," he ordered gruffly.

Whispers around them said, "Too bad. He's the worst one here. They'll be lucky to leave with anything in their hands."

But when they got to his station, he told them to take their packages and go. He checked nothing. On the bus more than half the passengers' packages had been taken away, but ours had been protected.

Virginia and Mike didn't have an address for the families, but before their departure, God gave Virginia a dream. She saw herself meeting Sister Lidia in front of the hotel. We later learned that Sister Lidia had the same dream.

At 7:00 a.m. the two women met, weeping with joy. Virginia and Mike returned home, joyfully reporting their successful journey. Later, we received a letter from Sister Lidia thanking us for our help.

Life in the Communist world is very hard, and the closer a person walks with God, the more difficult it becomes. After my children returned from Russia, the Lord opened a new way for me to transport Bibles from Romania all the way to Kisinov, Russia. Since I didn't know the person I was sending them to, I decided to go first and meet him.

Kisinov is built on the banks of the River Nistru. When I arrived at Kisinov, I realized that I was being followed by a Soviet policeman. Remembering God's protection, I was able to shake him off and make my way to some Christians. With them was a man named Visinov. After singing and praying for a time the Lord spoke to me through him. He said, "You must come before Me with fasting and prayer because you are going to go through a big trial and a mighty shaking. I am speaking to you before this happens so in the day of testing you will not be discouraged."

After we had prayed, I heard a miraculous story of a group of Christians who had been in Siberia. They had been forcibly taken there with their families and left without food. They had only shotguns for hunting, and tools with which to hew trees. Their orders were, "Cut down the forest."

After the police abandoned them there, they built a huge fire and slept beside it until morning. Then they began to dig a great hole. They cut down the trees and made a home for themselves in the dugout. They killed bears for food and used the skins for clothing.

For several years these courageous Christian believers had lived very primitively. They had nothing but meat to eat. The children began to grow hair on their bodies like animals. Without medicines, they could only turn to the Lord for healing. When the police returned expecting to find them all dead, they were stunned at the sight of a thriving village. A few days later they brought back food and medicine.

Eventually, Secretary Brezhnev's wife personally pleaded for their release. Her brother was among the exiled. When the laws were changed and the Christians were brought back home, they faced an unusual challenge.

Brother Visinov told me that he was better off *spiritually* in the forest. "I could praise God freely there," he explained. "Here, the body is free but the spirit is bound."

Minutes later, five men suddenly rushed into our prayer meeting carrying a man who had been in an accident. He was in a coma, so we quickly anointed him with oil. God healed him instantly.

When I returned home, it wasn't long before a new shipment of Bibles arrived at my house. I hid them carefully under the corn, because I sensed something bad was going to happen that night.

The next day a car full of policemen came to my house and searched for hours. I could see that God had closed their eyes, because they passed right by the Bibles and didn't see them. Nevertheless I was terrified.

They checked the house again, and again headed toward the area where the Bibles were stored. "Let's forget it," one of them finally said. "We've checked everything and we've got nothing to book him on."

I felt like shouting with joy, but managed to restrain myself.

Three days later, I was taken by the police and ordered not to have any communication with foreigners or with my own Christian countrymen. "If you do," they threatened me, "we'll do it the hard way. You'll be in jail, and you'll be very, very sorry."

When I returned to the house, I knew I was in serious trouble. My family joined me as I fasted and prayed, asking God for protection. In the days that followed I became more and more conscious of policemen following me. Although I continued to transport Bibles and to keep in touch with the missionaries, I felt a new, keen sadness.

God had warned me. Grave difficulties lay ahead.

MY DAUGHTER, VIRGINIA, AND HER HUSBAND, MIKE
- photo taken 1989 -

MY HOME IN HINSESTI, ROMANIA
- photo taken in 1989 -

Chapter Six

THE BEGINNING OF SORROWS

Day after day, I continued to sense impending difficulties. But one other matter still stirred in my heart. Were our Bibles being safely delivered once they arrived inside Russia? Were the Christians doing well there? Somehow I felt I had to see for myself. I asked God to give me and opportunity to visit the Soviet Union.

My heartfelt desire was to visit some of Russia's Christians. This seemed impossible because there would have to be other purposes for my trip as far as the authorities were concerned. So, by invitation, I joined Brother Adrian for a group tour.

I fasted and prayed for God's leadership. One of the heavy trials I always faced was the financial cost of transporting the Bibles. In spite of the difficulties, God enabled me to pay my own way, and then blessed me further by allowing me to give to others.

Eventually, I was forced to leave my job with the Fishing Department. They said a Communist should have the position. So I bought some pregnant minks from some Brothers in Russia. I took them home and began to raise mink to sell to the government. This furnished a good income for my family and ministry. Through this income I was able to help many. I had many fines to pay because of foreigners who came to us and were caught. They were simply sent from the country. Then the authorities came looking for me. Sometimes I didn't even know the people.

Once in the group tour in Russia, I went calling on a local Russian mayor in Kisinov, asking permission to "visit some historical churches". To my satisfaction, the necessary documents were provided.

Memories of Russia's Christian heritage stirred in me as I traveled from one ancient church to another. During one particular tour, I realized that I was being followed by someone... no doubt a soviet policeman. This disturbed me because I intended to stop on my way back to my hotel to see a Christian man named George, who Brother Bernard had told me about. "God help me," I prayed silently, wondering what I should do.

Just then a taxi pulled up and stopped. "Hey, Mister, do you want to go somewhere?"

"Yes!" I answered without a thought, and jumped into the cab.

"Where do you want to go?" he asked.

"I don't know!"

He looked puzzled. "Where are we going?"

"Wherever God leads us."

He pulled over to the right and said, "Get out, you're crazy! Where is your God?"

I said, "He is on the front of the car."

He said, "I don't see anything."

I said, "That's alright — I can see him. Just go where I tell you to go."

In a few minutes the angel on the hood had directed me to Brother George's home. I paid the driver and rang Brother George's doorbell. Though we had never met, we thanked God for giving us the opportunity of meeting!

When we had finished praying, I told George that I had come with money for needy Russian families, who were to meet me at the hotel. "But first," I asked, "did the Bibles which I sent, arrive safely?"

"Ycs," he answered, "the Bibles got through just fine, but we need many more."

Then he related how a group of Christians had been forced out of Kisinov. They had been driven a distance of thirty kilometers to a deserted place with no food and no means of getting any. This hurt me deeply. "I want to meet with these people!"

George took me to a local prayer meting where they were already in prayer, asking God to show them where the Christians George had told me about were. We joined them in prayer. After a time, God gave one of them a vision, showing where they were. We agreed to leave right away to see if we could find them, and check out the situation.

We left Kisinov and arrived in the area between Kisinov and Odessa - called "Black Valley" - about 2:00 a.m.. We verified the needs, then returned to Kisinov.

That same day we gathered clothing, food, and money to take back. Then I returned to the hotel. We had to repack our suitcases with clothing to give away.

Hoping not to be detected, we left for the "Black Valley" early the next morning, with two cars full of clothing.

The Secret Police followed us and were about to overtake us. "God," we cried out in prayer, "don't let them catch us! Don't let them kill us!"

We thought we were as good as caught, but just then, a huge black cloud came up over us. Soon it began to rain. We were driving into a slow, easy rain, but behind was a torrential downpour, hail and all! The violent cloudburst broke the police car's windshield and stopped their pursuit instantly.

Because of the rain, the unpaved road became so muddy we soon had to stop our cars. We got out, picked up the suitcases and began to walk. Suddenly we heard noises ahead of us. We froze in our tracks, not knowing who was about to appear. But a group of youngsters appeared and offered to help carry our suitcases.

Certainly we had been surprised to see the youngsters coming to help us. But we were even more surprised to learn that all those faithful believers had stayed awake awaiting our arrival!

In spite of the relentless rain, their faces shone bright as the sun. An old man about 60 years old welcomed us. "Thank God!" he rejoiced. "Everything He has shown me has come true. We have been praying for help and last night as we prayed, the Holy Spirit let us know that you were coming!"

We were quite joyful. But best of all, the Christians of Kisinov now knew where these people were, and someone would be able to aid them from time to time.

After about an hour of warm and powerful prayer, we gave the clothing and food to Ioan, the old man who had foretold our arrival. "Hand it out to everyone," I instructed him, "and pray that God will help me return as soon as possible." With that, we departed.

On the way home we were stopped at a Police road block.

"Which one of you is Dumitru Duduman?" they demanded.

"I'm the one you're looking for," I answered.

"Come with us."

Relieved that I was the only one taken, I soon found myself at the police station. The Chief of Police spoke good Romanian. "If you came to Russia to visit, what are you doing spending your time with Christians? Don't you know better than that?"

I could hear others being beaten in another room. I knew I would probably be next, but the Lord gave me strength. "Why are you holding me here?" I asked. "Take me to the President. I want to talk to him."

When they heard this they started talking to each other in Russian. "What should we do with him?" they asked each other.

Finally the commander ordered everyone to go home except for one officer who was to stay with me. After about an hour I asked him in Romanian, "Are you going to hold me here longer?"

"I don't know what you are saying because I do not speak Romanian," he answered in Russian.

In Russian I answered, "Are you sure you don't speak Romanian? If you don't, no problem. I speak Russian."

When he heard me speaking Russian, he looked at me fearfully and went outside. I was left alone. I waited for someone else to come. As I was sitting there not knowing what to do, I heard a familiar voice.

"Go to the hotel."

I knew it was the angel's voice, but before I left I looked in all the rooms, yelling, "Where are you guys? I'm leaving!" I saw no one so I returned to the hotel. I prayed and went to sleep. In a short while two policemen arrived and told me I would have to leave the next day. (Later, some Christians came to check on me, but I was already gone.)

I couldn't sleep that night. I was concerned that I was going to miss the ones I had brought the clothes and money for. But during prayer, the voice of the Lord told me it was going to be alright, that they would be there before I had to leave. Sure enough, at about 5:00 a.m. I was in front of the hotel and there was Lidia and Anna, wives of some of the pastors that had been exiled. They had the sad news that instead of their husbands being released from prison, their sentences had increased. After they left, I caught my train to Kiev.

In Kiev I went to my room and prayed that God would guide me. "Lead me, Lord... protect me." I raised my hands before the Lord and said, "I can do all things through Christ who strengthens me." I slept soundly until morning. But when I awoke, I couldn't get out of bed, and we were to see more sights that day!

What was wrong with me? The tour guide worriedly called a doctor. When he arrived with two male nurses, he asked my name. I told him, "Dumitru Duduman." I noticed one of them acted a little strange when I said my name. The doctor gave me a shot and bandaged my leg saying he would be back in three hours. They left and I went immediately to sleep. When the door bell rang I jumped out of bed. My leg didn't hurt anymore. I went to the door and when I opened it, only the doctor was there. He said, "Peace of God to you, Brother, my name is Emil. I am the pastor of a Baptist church here and God let me know I would meet you at the hotel." Putting his hand on my shoulder he told me all the Bibles had arrived safely and he was the one in charge of them. We prayed together, then embraced each other and he left. I didn't know that I would ever see him again but the next day he came and took me to visit the city and some churches. He also took me to visit some brethren who worked with Bibles and some places where churches had been destroyed. During this time we were able to discuss how to get Bibles into Russia in greater quantities. He, being a doctor, gave us liberty to go to some places without question, but he told me about the seven churches with gold domes. That part of the Soviet Union had once belonged to Romania and these churches were built by the Romanians.

My tour guide, who spoke Romanian, was a young woman from a Christian family. I was anxious to see the loving tributes to God that had been so skillfully created by my ancestors. This land had been given to Romania when a Russian prince married a Romanian princess. The gift had included Cernauti, Kisinov, Odessa and part of Kiev. In 1944 the Russians came in by force and took back the land they gave and even more. Now many Romanians live in that territory, which is Moldavia.

When we arrived at the first church in Kiev, my guide gave me a paper that authorized my entry. We were checked and allowed to go inside. As we entered the gate, we found ourselves in a breathtakingly lovely garden, lavish with trees and flowers. The church gleamed in the light. In front was a marker stating the church had been built by Stephen the Great in Gratitude to God for seven separate victories over the Turks in one single year. After absorbing the quiet solitude of the garden, we went into the church. But, instead of seeing symbols of faith and emblems of Christ's life, death and resurrection - to my shock and sadness - there were only pictures of Communist leaders; Lenin, Stalin, Marx and others.

"Once the walls of this church were covered with priceless things; memories of our ancestors," my guide quietly explained. "But one day those were taken out and pictures of the Soviet President and members of the Party were put up instead."

How my heart ached when I heard this.

My guide motioned with her hand. "Come, I will show you a place where you might be a little happier." We made our way to the River Nipru. On the river bank was a statue bearing the name of John the Baptist. I was surprised. I

91

asked Lenuta, the guide, "Why do the Communists allow this statue to be here?" She smiled, "Well, they never wanted to leave it, that's for sure. A lot of people tried to destroy the statue, but everyone who tried, died. Some people bombarded it with tanks, but that didn't work either, because the shells from the tank ricocheted back at them."

Lenuta pointed out the crosses around the statue. "Those are the graves of those who tried to destroy the statue. Through this, God has put fear in the hearts of the enemy. Instead of destroying it, now they take care of it!"

Somewhat inspired, I returned to my hotel and as I entered, I had to show my passport. The man checking my documents said, "I want to tell you something. You'd better be careful. The Romanian police have reported that you are a Christian spy. We have orders to follow you."

I thanked him and shook his hand. "I am a Christian too," he said softly. "But don't tell anybody."

In the morning I telephoned Brother Teofil, whose number I had, and asked him to meet me in my room. When he arrived he had another Brother with him who was helping smuggle Bibles. They didn't stay long for fear of being arrested and their families being taken away. I also was trembling, so we went on our knees in prayer. As we prayed I had a vision. I saw a great light, and in that light was a man dressed in white with a shining belt around His waist. He was standing with His hands stretched out. He looked at me and said, "Dumitru, I will suffer in your place because I am used to suffering. Look at my hands." I saw they were bleeding. A bolt of terror shot through me. I was terrified - gripped with emotion - as I gazed into the Heavenly face! "Don't be afraid," the voice continued. "I will be with you and you will be victorious." Then the vision ended.

When we finished praying, the young man with Brother

Teofil said, "Brother Dumitru, don't be discouraged. I want to tell you what has happened to me."

Stelica, just twenty-four years old, had longed in his heart to find a wife who was God's choice for him. He had fasted and prayed fervently. The next day he had written on scraps of paper the names of all the churches he knew about. Then he had drawn one. On the following Sunday he walked to the church whose name he had drawn. He talked to the pastor and asked to enter the church early - before anyone else arrived. The pastor agreed. When he entered, he found a seat, sat down and waited.

"Lord," he prayed, "please let the first girl to come into the church be the one You have chosen to be my wife." Stelica sat nervously, awaiting the girl's arrival. When she walked in, he was touched by the peace he saw on her face, and by the way she sang every song by heart. But she never looked his way.

After the service, Stelica boldly stood up and told the congregation that he wanted the girl's hand. To his shock she didn't turn to look at him, but the mother stood and began to tearfully speak. He learned that Mary, the lovely girl who had entered the church first, was blind.

Nevertheless Stelica had believed that Mary was God's choice for him. He asked her and her mother for her hand, and after many tears and discussion between the mother, his family, and the pastor, they all agreed.

So Stelica invited me to the wedding. It would take place the day before I was to leave Russia. At nine that morning, Brother Teofil arrived to take me to the wedding. It was a day of joy, and God's presence was in our midst. A surprising number of people were there because the occasion had been publicized by the Communists. A Christian was marrying a blind girl. Some were crying because of the tragic condition of the bride. I was asked to speak, and under the guidance of the Spirit of God I spoke in faith. "God is able to do a miracle here that will make our joy complete."

At 11:30 a.m. the ceremony started. After my words, the pastor prayed for the couple, asking God's blessing upon the marriage. As they prayed, the bride began to speak. Her first words were, "Oh, God, what a beautiful dress I am wearing. I can see what a handsome husband I have... I can see!"

What a marvelous moment it was when we realized that God had given her eyesight! Everyone was ecstatically thanking God for the miracle. When she was asked to pray, Mary said, "God, I thank you for this day. You were the first guest at our wedding and You have given me the most wonderful wedding gift I could have ever imagined. Thank You for our new life, thank you from the bottom of my heart that You have given me my eyesight. Thank You for giving me such a handsome husband. Even though I was blind, he wanted to marry me. God, You have brought so much joy to me, I can never thank You enough. Dear God, never let me forget what You have done."

Stelica said his love for Mary had continually grown stronger as the wedding day approached.

A government cameraman, who was at the wedding to take pictures, ran away after the miracle happened, and no more publicity was given to the marriage. This happened in 1980.

After that joyful event I went back home and found my family safe, welcoming me home with open arms. But the very next day, while I was helping Maria prepare breakfast on an outdoor stove, I saw a police car stop in front of the house. Fear pounded in my heart. I remembered the vision I'd had in Russia. Somehow I understood from that moment on that hard times had begun.

Five officers got out of the car. One of them roughly said, "Mr. Duduman, we have some complaints against you. We understand that you are working with foreigners and with Bibles. That is why we've come to check all of your property. Wc have a warrant from the court."

They stood Maria and me with our faces against the wall, and started to check the house. They began to check it at 8:00 a.m. and finished at 4:00 p.m.

Virginia had been home only one day, just 8 days after giving birth to her second son, Sergiu Dumitru. Her Husband (Mike), and first son (also Mike) were not home at the time. Because Virginia was ill and weak (with a temperature of 100+ degrees), the police allowed her to stay in her room.

Meanwhile, they ripped apart our books, pillows, closets, and clothes. They even broke Virginia's guitar in a rough attempt to search inside it. By the time they finished, the house was in tctal chaos. They stacked all the religious books on the table. "We'll take these with us!" they said. But they did not find any bibles. God's protection was with us.

"That is my literature and you can't take it away!" I told them firmly.

After checking everything in the house, they went outside and began snooping around. When I saw them going toward the bicycle, I became so worried I couldn't move a muscle. But they found nothing!

Then, one of the Policemen was ordered to search the barn. When he headed toward the barn my worry increased, because I knew there were thousands of Bibles fitted between the rafters of the attic, and covered with hay. He searched the main floor, then climbed the ladder to check the attic. But when he started to walk in the attic, it began to creak and move from all the weight in it. Not knowing the weight of the Bibles was causing the movement, he became frightened , and said, "There's nothing up here! I'm not going to make this old barn collapse and kill me for no good reason!"

We had other hiding places around our home, which I was not concerned about. For example: to one side of our home, we had a small garden. Every year we would plant an area of corn especially for hiding Bibles.

In the beginning, we dug large holes in the area where the corn would be planted. We then set 50 gallon plastic containers into the holes. Next, we filled each container with Bibles, put the lids on them, covered them with dirt and planted the corn. From then on, whenever we needed to access the Bible storage, we would go out at night, dig up the corn, retrieve or add Bibles and replant the corn.

After they finished their search, they closed their report and made Virginia and me sign it. Then I walked outside with them, and they left.

When I returned, I said, "I don't understand how the Bibles on the bicycle disappeared." Virginia told me she had remembered I had 3 suitcases of Bibles strapped to the bicycle behind the house. Virginia wanted to move the Bibles, but didn't want to be followed. She came into the room where we were being held, and asked for permission to go to the outhouse which was also located behind our home. They allowed her to go alone. When Virginia was behind the house, she managed to remove the heavy Bibles from the bicycle. It was with much difficulty that she managed to hide the Bibles near the river further behind the house. Because she was so weak, she would struggle two or three steps, and fall. By the time she returned to the house, she was much worse, but God was with her. She made it safely back to the house without being caught by the police.

Our family fell on our knees in prayer, thanking God for His deliverance. While we were praying the angel of God appeared. "I came to tell you to be strong and trust in the Lord. You will soon go through more trials, beatings and torture. Don't be afraid, I will be with you. I will give you the victory. Just be careful that you don't reveal anything to your tormenters. Don't confess to anything - no matter what they do or ask!"

After he finished, there was a bright light and a loud sound, then he vanished.

I got to my feet and said to myself, "God can do whatever He wants with me. How can I say 'No' to anything He wants me to do? If God has decided I should go through trials, then so be it." I felt sure that God would eventually give me the victory, just as the angel promised. But it wasn't easy. How I dreaded being in the hands of the police again!

On the sixth of July, I awoke to a great uneasiness - a heavy sadness. Although I couldn't explain my feelings of dread, they stayed with me all day. About 10:00 p.m. a man who worked for the police came to the door. "Mr. Duduman," he said, "tomorrow at 8 a.m. you have to be at the police station and report to Captain Sandru." My deep sorrow increased.

I couldn't sleep, but I chose not to tell Maria and the children what was happening.

The next morning I made my way to the bus station, praying as I went. This was July 1980. I caught the bus for Suceava. When I got there, I reported to Captain Sandru.

I was taken to a room and ordered to confess. "You have been reported for having dealings with foreigners and for transporting Bibles." The policeman said they had proof

97

of my "*crimes*". He began to read from a letter which they had received from a Christian, giving every detail of my Bible smuggling activities, including what I had eaten for breakfast, lunch and dinner! It said we had gone fishing; had given him fried fish to take home; and a jar of jam for his wife. Perhaps most tragically of all, Brother Dieg's name was included in the letter. They asked about every Christian author of literature they had wanted to confiscate.

"Because you are a christian, you HAVE to tell us the truth!" They asked how Bibles were transported, what Christian foreigners I knew and what meetings I had attended. But as far as my responses were concerned, I might as well have been deaf and dumb.

When they observed my silence, they began kicking me - spitting in my face - beating me!

"If you are a Christian, why don't you ask your God to save you from our hands - from the hands of the Devil?" they jeered.

After they beat me until I was unconscious, they threw cold water on me, then started beating me again.

For five months this agony continued. It seemed to me that those days would never end. They would torture me for days, to the point of death, then send me home to recuperate. As soon as I was able to function somewhat reasonably, they would arrest me again, and repeat the cycle. My family and I were desperate. But by His grace, I kept my promise to God. And His Holy Spirit let me know that I would surely be victorious.

During one of my times at home, I made the difficult decision to confront Pop Liviu, the man who had written the letter about me and the missionaries.

When I arrived at his house in Cluj, He was defenseless. He didn't know what to say to me or how to get rid of me.

"Do you realize what you have done?" I cornered him

with frustrating questions. "Do you see what the Devil has made of you? Aren't you afraid of the day when you will be asked by God why you did this? The day will come when you will have to answer for all the terrible things you have done!"

While I was talking, Liviu's son-in-law walked through the door. I heard God's whisper in my ear, "Get out of here as fast as you can." I rose quickly and rushed out. I had to walk about five kilometers to the train station.

While the train was approaching the city of Suceava where I had to catch the bus, the angel of the Lord spoke to me and told me not to get off at Suceava. "The police are waiting for you. Be alert because the Lord will protect you in a way you don't think possible."

I thanked the Lord and decided to stop at the station past Suceava, in Bucecea. When we passed Suceava, I saw three policemen standing on the platform. How tragic it would have been for me to have been arrested without my family's knowledge.

I rode another half hour to Veresti, where I had to change trains. When I started to get off, I felt a hand pull me back. Suddenly, the train I needed to board moved along side and I was able to get on it without being seen. After about twenty minutes the train stopped for a light. "Get off here!" I heard the Lord direct me. "The police are at the station." I got off. At that moment the train started again.

I walked home through the corn fields, unseen. It was wet because it had rained but, finally, I got home. When I arrived, I found Maria in tears. "I was worried sick about you because ever since you left, the police have been looking for you. Worse than that, police officers are stationed at our neighbors' houses, watching for you!"

"Maria, we just have to trust God. We will be

victorious, and we need to thank God for all He does for us."

I ate dinner and went to bed. It grew late, but I couldn't sleep. Our dog kept barking angrily, and I knew from the sound of his bark that someone was snooping around. Someone was searching for me - right outside our house!

THE POLICE STATION WHERE I WAS INTERROGATED
AND TORTURED SO MANY TIMES

Chapter Seven

A MATTER OF LIFE AND DEATH

At 5:30 a.m., a messenger from the police department pounded on the front door. "Report to the colonel at 7:00 a.m.," he snapped, turning on his heels and marching off.

I got dressed. After prayer I said goodbye to my family and headed for the bus station.

My heart ached so badly when I left the house that I couldn't even look back. Upon arriving at Suceava I had to walk about fifteen minutes. I felt so weak and weary that I could hardly place one foot in front of the other. Then, when I finally arrived, no one was there to let me in.

Within my heart I heard a familiar voice, "Didn't I tell you not to be afraid? So many times I have been with you and you have been victorious. Now throw away your fear and believe me fully. Jesus is your Savior. Don't testify to anything they ask you. Just remember the blood that He shed for you and for all the world. This is your salvation."

When I entered the police station, I went to the second floor. I entered an office where there were a number of chairs. Feelings no strength at all, I sat on one of the chairs. No sooner did I sit, without even a moment to catch my breath, than a door swung open and a sturdily built man with a mustache appeared, looking furious. I heard him call

101

my name. "I am Colonel Voinea," he barked at me, "and I have been assigned to your case. I am quite sure that what my colleagues couldn't get out of you I will. You will even tell me what you DON'T know. Don't worry, Duduman, I'll take care of you!"

He then got right into my face and growled, "Tell me where you were and why!" I did not answer his question. He slapped me and I fell to the floor. He then began to kick me with his boots, not looking where he kicked.

My mind flashed to the memory of a young Christian who had recently died, having been kicked repeatedly in the liver. "God help me!" I cried out silently.

He was enraged. "Now will you tell me?" he repeated time and again.

I shook my head, no.

"Don't worry," he would say. "Don't worry, you'll tell me." He continued to kick me until he grew tired.

Then, two different colonels beat me. There may have been others, but I actually don't remember. I only know that I carry scars in my body today which continue to cause me pain - herniated wounds caused form the blows of the boots.(The Romanian Secret Police wear boots like the Nazi SS wore - made specificallly for human torture!)

I began to vomit and lost consciousness. When I woke up they put me in a very small cement room with spikes protruding from the walls to keep prisoners from leaning. There was not enough room to sit down, so I had to stand.

The floor was a grate of iron bars and the cold river water flowed over the bars across my bare feet. There was also water dripping slowly from above, onto my head. After some time, my head became completely numb. My legs became swollen.

I have no idea how long I was there, but when they took me from the cell I was so weak I collapsed. They said,

"Oh, your legs are blue! You are cold! We'll warm you up!"

Looking at me with contempt, they strapped me around the waist, lifted me up, suspended me in the air and beat my feet with rubber hoses. "You're a Christian! You MUST tell us the truth! We'll show you what kind of a God is making you keep information from us! Will He take you out of our hands?"

One of them began hitting me in the head with the butt of his rifle. I was cut and bleeding. I passed out again. When I began to come to, I could feel that my eyes were covered with blood. I didn't want to open them for fear that I could not see. Besides, if they saw I was coming to, they would beat me again.

I prayed what I thought was a final prayer, "God, I know I'm dying. If I've done anything wrong or if I have displeased You in any way, please forgive me. And, please take care of my wife and daughter."

I heard someone coming. I didn't move a muscle; I was waiting for the end. This time I could not escape. But I was mistaken. The man did not strike me. Instead I heard him say, "You will not leave here until you tell me who brings you the Russian Bibles and where you take them. What foreigners do you know? What is your relationship with them? What other Romanians are involved with these foreigners? I will make you tell me everything I have asked you!"

When he left, the voice spoke to me again. "Don't be afraid, because the time is short. I will not leave you, but will remain at your side. Don't worry about what to say because I will put the right words in your mouth."

After two days in that room without food or water, another colonel came and took me to his office. He introduced himself as Colonel Sandru and began asking me all kinds of questions, none of which I answered. When he saw I wouldn't tell him anything, he started hitting me with a club which had metal prongs attached to it's end. Every time it struck my head it left me bloody. He hit me half a dozen times in the head and arm. Then he left, locking me in his office.

I thought to myself, "I have been put in jail; I have been beat up. Now all that is left is for me to die - for them to kill me. "God," I pleaded, "I have worked for You, and now You've allowed me to fall into the Communist's hands. Why must I be tortured like this?" But when I was in my darkest hour, a light appeared in the room and a loud voice said, "Be strong! Strengthen yourself! I came to be your help and to be with you."

"Who are you?"

"I am the angel, Gabriel, the Commander of the Heavenly Army. I was sent to protect you; to keep you from being afraid. They will come in a short time to take you away from here. Don't tell them anything or write anything down for them."

In a few moments, a colonel entered the office and told me to come with him. He took me to his office and said, "There on the table is a piece of paper and a pen. Sit down and write everything you know." I sat in the chair and wrote, "Out of all the questions I have been asked, I do not know the answer to even one of them." Then I signed my name - "Duduman, Dumitru" - and put the pen down.

The colonel snatched the paper off the table and scanned it. When he saw there was nothing, he became infuriated. He hit me with his fists. He kicked me. He spat on me and said, "You are still holding out and you don't want to tell us anything. You say you don't know. Okay. Well, after I get through with you, you will remember everything!"

After beating me again, he gave me another piece of

paper and told me to write. I didn't finish writing because, when Colonel Voinea saw I was writing the same thing over and over, he started hitting me and slamming my head on the table. Then he took me to the door, stuck my fingers in the crack and slammed it. He also poked pins under my fingernails and said, "You are still acting smart. Listen, if you don't start talking, it will be all over for you. You'll see what will happen."

He held my fingers in the door while he kicked me in the back. I didn't know what to do, the pain was so intense. I could feel tears rolling down my cheeks, but still I said nothing. He beat me until he got tired and left. Another one came and took me back to my cell. Day after day they tried different tactics, using different measures of torture. They attempted all kinds of clever "experiments", but their most repeated torment was simply to beat me until I fainted. As usual, they threw cold water on me until I regained consciousness. Then they resumed the beating again.

When I look back at all this, I know that God shortened the days or I would have died. God kept me alive. Only His strength brought me through victoriously.

One day I was taken from my cell to an office where there were seven people, all of them policemen. Each of them had the rank of captain or colonel. Colonel Voinea, who was responsible for my case, told me in a very harsh voice, "Listen, if you don't write what you know about these Bibles and foreign missionaries, I give you my word in front of my colleagues, I will finish you off!"

I was left alone momentarily, and I heard voices from the room next to me. I was able to distinguish my wife's voice, and others which were yelling at her. It sounded like they were beating her. Then the sounds stopped. I thought they sent her home.

Then the policemen returned. "Listen, Dumitru,"

Colonel Voinea said, "Maria has told us everything, and we have sent her home. Now, YOU just tell also, and we'll let you go home, too."

"If Maria knows, she knows. I don't know anything. But, if she has already told you, why are you asking me?" I said.

"So you conspired together about what to say to us, did you?"

I was puzzled by what he said, but he didn't give me time to think long. *(Maria would later explain to me what the colonel had meant.)*

"Now, start writing!" the officer ordered me. Although I was afraid, I did not write anything that would appeal to the Colonel's tastes. When Voinea saw that I was writing the same thing as before, he became very angry and started hitting me so hard I thought I could not stand the pain.

When I came to, the angel was there, again. When at last I could see, I noticed a doctor was injecting a needle into me. "Don't make a big commotion. You already have nine broken ribs. Stay still and let me take care of you. If you move it will cause internal bleeding and that will kill you."

After the doctor taped my ribs, they sent me home. It was evening when I left the Police station. I had to walk to the bus stop. Because of the beating, I struggled to get there before the last bus left. I barely made it on time.

When the bus stopped near my home, I was so stiff, I was unable to even get out. Some men with a wagon at the bus stop helped me off the bus, into the wagon, and took me home.

When I arrived, the men helped me into the house and into bed - but Maria was not there! I asked Virginia where she was.

"Five policemen came this morning and took her with

them. I was terrified!" she said.

So was I. In a weak voice, I cried out to God, "God, after all the beatings and tortures I have gone through, now will You let them take my wife and beat her, too?" I felt that I could bear no more. I was angry and had no more strength in my body. I couldn't do anything. My grief was so great that I couldn't eat. I lay on my bed but could find no peace. I wanted to sleep but my physical and emotional pain wouldn't let me.

Virginia, seeing my situation, wept bitterly, begging me to eat something.

"I'm not hungry," I told her.

"What hurts you so much, Father? Please tell me what those barbarians did to you. Your body is nearly destroyed!"

It was true. That IS what I was — destroyed! I felt I could not live one more day.

I had been home about six hours and still Maria had not returned. I became more and more upset. Three MORE hours of worry and agonizing passed before I finally saw the door open. (It was well after midnight by then.) In came Maria. When she stepped inside, she collapsed. She was pale and yellow; her eyes were red and swollen from crying. But, she had not expected to find me at home. When she saw me, she screamed with joy, "Oh! I'm so glad you're home!" It was as if she'd forgotten her own misery.

I was happy, too, and said, "Thank God, He's helped me to see my family again." I asked her what the police did to her and she said, "When I got there this morning, they were very rude. They began to yell at me and one of them reached his hand out to hit me. But before having a chance to do it again, I became sick, and they began to treat me nicely. But, they had a lot of questions about you and many others. I had, only one answer to each question and that was, 'I don't know'. They said you had already told them all of the answers to the questions, and they had sent you home. They said they just wanted me to answer them also, and they would send me home, too. I simply told them, 'If Dumitru knows, he knows. I don't know anything. But, if he has already told you, why are you asking me?'" *(Then I knew why the colonel had accused Maria and me of conspiring about what we were going to tell them.)*

Maria went on, "They kept me in interrogation until it was dark outside, telling me that if I would confess they would let you go home. They saw I wouldn't break so they released me. Since it was after 8:00 p.m., the busses weren't running any more. I had to walk home the whole 18 kilometers through the forest."

I was so thankful that she was finally home. I said, "Let's pray together. We need to thank God for what He has done for us."

We fell to our knees in prayer; all of us crying. The Spirit of God was heavy upon us and the angel showed himself again and told me that my sufferings were not ended yet, but my victory would be soon. He said, "You will go through one more wave of trial. It will be the hardest, but you must say the same thing you have said. Don't change your answer, and God will guide you and save you."

At first I didn't receive the angel's words well. They only seemed to promise more suffering and anguish. I thought, "What is man that he should stand in the way of God?" I did not know that, through my suffering, God would be exalted. He would also make believers of those who did not acknowledge His existence.

My family and I joined with some other Christians who shared my grief and sorrows. As one, we began to fast and pray. I wanted to be filled with more power from God, so

I asked for it repeatedly.

At the end of six days of prayer and fasting, about 8:00 a.m., a police car pulled up and I was arrested again.

Crying aloud, I left the house and my loved ones who also wept bitterly. Clearly, God's plans couldn't be changed.

I got into the car where three officers awaited me. Within half an hour we were at the police station again. I was taken to the man I wanted least in all the world to see - Colonel Voinea. He had no heart, no mercy. He could hardly wait to start beating me again. He sneered at me. "Oh, so you came, Saint. Let's see what you will tell me now! I think maybe this time you will tell me what you ate ten years ago! All of your so-called 'Brothers' have told me everything. You are the only one who keeps strong in his faith and doesn't want to tell. If you love life and your family you will tell us everything you know."

He gave me a chair and told me to sit down. He then gave me a paper and pen and told me to "...write everything that you know referring to Bibles, meetings with foreigners, people that communicate where the Bibles are - everything to do with your work." I wrote the same thing I wrote before, only this time I wrote in capital letters, "I DON'T KNOW ANYONE WHO BRINGS MESSAGES ABOUT FOREIGN LITERATURE."

When the colonel saw he was not getting anything out of me, he left the room for a while. Then he returned with Brother Vasile Hacman from Radauti, to see if we knew each other. Of course we knew each other very well, but we pretended not to recognize one another. Colonel Voinea asked, "Do you know this man?"

"How should I know him?" I asked. "Maybe I saw him sometime, but there are a lot of Christians. How can I remember them all?"

Then he said to Brother Vasile, "Do you know

Duduman?" He shook his head that he didn't know me.
When I remember how Brother Vasile Hacman looked, I am
still terrified. The poor man had been beaten up so badly
that even his eyes seemed to be lost in all the swelling.

Seeing he could get nothing from us, he took Brother
Vasile out and brought in Brother Ion from Danila. Colonel
Voina said, "Duduman, Don't try to tell me you don't know
Ion. He told me he knows you."

"Even if he says he knows me, I don't know him."

At that point Brother Ion was taken out and three other
Christians came in. They were from Poeana Sibiului. I didn't
know them, nor had I ever seen them, but Colonel Voinea
wanted to make us say we knew each other. He spat out,
"Hey! Why don't you just tell the truth? I found your
address in one of their pockets and I caught them with two
cars full of Bibles which they were obviously taking to you."

"Maybe they were taking them to my house, but I don't
remember ever seeing them."

The Brothers didn't know ME <u>this</u> time either, so he
still had no answer. He motioned with his hand and took
them to another room. I was left alone for a few minutes.
"God," I prayed, "how much longer do I have to suffer?"

The hurting seemed to grow more and more. Nobody
cared that I was suffering badly. I was black and blue, with
nine broken ribs. They only wanted to hurt me more.

Then another cruel officer, Colonel Presteniuc entered
the picture. He had no fear of God and wanted to destroy
me, but it seemed to be God's wish for this officer to take
over my case. Like a madman, he burst through the door
with my file in his hand! He looked at me, spat in my face
and swore. "I will not put up with you! I will kill you
because I hate all Christians and have no patience with you!
Nothing we've tried has worked! I'll give you one more
chance to change your mind..."

I said nothing, hoping not to anger him more. Seeing I didn't respond, he motioned for me to follow him. He took me to a dark room in which there was an odd-looking chair with some straps and wiring attached. I hardly had a chance to think about what it all meant when Colonel Presteniuc said, "This time you can say goodbye to your life because I am about to electrocute you!"

Just then I heard the voice of the Lord in my ear saying, "Don't be afraid. I am with you and you won't die."

I was surprised and happy that the angel of God was with me. The Colonel told me to sit on the chair and said, "I can't do anything about this. You are the one who pushed me this far because you will not tell anything. Now all this equipment will tell everything." Roughly, he began attaching cuffs and electrodes to me; two of them in my ears and one at my heart. Some sort of metal hood device fit over my head. He said, "Now it's time to remember where you took the Bibles and what foreigners you know." Then he turned on a light that was about ten times brighter than normal, and fixed it over my head. As soon as he turned on the light, the appliances attached to the chair began to produce a very loud sound. When all this began, the angel appeared in front of me, dressed in a shiny white robe. "Don't be afraid," he said. "The Lord will be with you and won't leave you. Remember - don't think of anything except the blood of Jesus. The authorities will be left ashamed!" He then disappeared.

I did as the angel had instructed me and thought only about the blood of Jesus. This only lasted a little while because the light, the noise and the electrical current soon caused me to pass out. I don't know how long I was unconscious, but when I woke up I was being drenched with water and slapped. This process seemed to be repeated all day.

The men around me cared nothing for my condition.

111

Every time I began to lose consciousness they soaked me and slapped me, trying to revive me.

When the ordeal was finally over, the Colonel was sure he had his information. He turned on his recorder. "Now we will hear the truth," he laughed. But when the tape began to play, all he heard was, "The blood of Jesus. The blood of Jesus. The blood of Jesus." He was furious!

"I can't understand why you would call upon the blood of Jesus. Why do you need Him now? The blood of Jesus cleansed you once when you became a Christian. I don't see why you should call on Him. Can't you see that you are in my hands now?"

With that, he left me in the room alone, locking the door behind him. He returned after a few hours, but seeing I was so incredibly weak, he told me to go home. "If you care about your family, don't tell anyone what I did to you... and be back here tomorrow morning at eight o'clock sharp!"

I tried to walk but was not able to. When they saw this, two policemen took me, put me in their car and drove me home. When we arrived home, they grabbed my legs and arms, and threw me on the porch in front of the house.

My family was devastated at the sight of me, but I didn't tell them anything. We got on our knees and prayed for God to take the pain and agony from me. We went to bed that night, but I couldn't sleep for fear of what would happen the next day. Finally I thought, "I will be strong until the end. Maybe, through my suffering, others will be saved. In any case, God will guide me."

At last I fell asleep. The next morning I took the bus back to the police station. "God," I prayed, "You know that my human strength is failing me. I feel weaker and weaker every time they attack me. Please give me the power to fight until the end."

I was at the police station at 8:00 a.m. and the colonel was waiting for me. He took me to the chair and started the whole process again. Because of the effect of the electricity, the bright light and the noise, I felt sick and passed out.

I don't know how long I was out, but when I came to, I was no longer in the chair. I was lying on the floor. Once again Presteniuc played the recording... "Blood of Jesus! Blood of Jesus."

He picked up the phone and called six policemen. They began to kick me with their boots. I heard him saying, "Kill him!" I passed out again.

When I awoke, a doctor was working over me. As I lay there expecting the colonel to return, someone hurried into the room and interrupted, "Doctor come quick! Colonel Presteniuc is dying!" They left quickly.

A few minutes later, another colonel entered. "I am Colonel Cerlinca," he said. "I came to tell you to go home. Come back tonight at 7:00 p.m., and tomorrow at 8:00 a.m.. Get dressed!"

"Why? Have you finished killing me?" I asked.

"Colonel Presteniuc is dead! Your God has given you true justice." Then he hesitated for a moment before he spoke. "But, please, don't pray to your God against ME. I never harmed you."

Then, because I could not get up, he helped me to my feet. He assisted me as I tried to dress myself, and provided support as I walked out into the hall. "Stay here until you feel better, then you can go." I sat in a chair and fell asleep. When I awoke, I realized that I was not dreaming but that I was free to go. I was so thankful that I was not being tortured. I asked God to give me the strength to get home.

As I was praying and leaning against the walls in order to get out of the place, a young policeman from our village stopped, took one look at me and cried out, "Oh my God!

What have they done to you?"

But I was too weak to explain anything to him.

"Don't you know anything about what has happened?" he asked.

"No. What?"

"At about 10:30 a.m., Colonel Presteniuc was standing in his office with your file in his hand. Suddenly he fell down and began to hemorrhage internally. When the doctor arrived, Presteniuc was dead. Now, all the other officers involved in your case are terrified!"

Another Colonel entered the room where we were. "You can go home now," he said. "You're free." Then he called two policemen to help me outside. They put me on a bus and sent me home.

Colonel Presteniuc was the hardest, most dangerous colonel they had. No one hated Christians more than he did.

114

Chapter Eight

HEARTBREAKS AND HEALINGS

After the surprising words of the young policeman, I somehow managed to reach my brother's house which was directly across the street from the bus station. His family was devastated when they saw me. I was bloody and sallow, my eyes sunken deep in my head. I could do no more than stare at them like a man in a stupor. Everyone cried, asking again and again, "What have they done to you?"

My brother sent word for Virginia to come and take me home. She struggled to help me, trying to get me to lean against her as we walked, but I was too heavy and weak. She quickly stopped a man with a horse and wagon, pleading with him to take me to the house.

When Maria saw me, she fainted. I could only lay in bed in this terrible condition, propped all around with pillows. My internal injuries made it impossible for me to eat anything but the smallest portions. I frequently vomited blood, and grew weaker all the time. Soon, I could no longer walk.

Weeks passed. Many missionaries came, but they just took pictures and left. Many Christian friends came to pray for me, but there was no improvement.

Throughout this time I often wondered if I was going

115

to die. I even asked God to take me home - my misery was so great. Virginia begged. "Father, don't give up! Don't die! We need you!"

Three months passed, and I was still bedfast. One night when I was sleeping, the angel of the Lord woke me. He spoke sharply to me and said, "Enough! Get out of bed. Go outside and walk around the house."

"Will you wait until I get back?"

"I will wait."

Jumping out of bed, I quickly went outside, ran around the house and came back in. The angel was still there. He said, "Are you still hurting?"

"No."

"Can you walk?"

"Yes."

"Then you will be smuggling Bibles for another four years. The police will be following you step-by-step, but they won't be able to catch you. After the four years are over, at 10:00 a.m., on July 22 1984, when they see they cannot convict you, you will be exiled from Romania, leaving your relatives and friends behind, and sent to America."

Then he disappeared, and the room was dark. I knew that I was not dreaming. But I also knew that I wasn't the only one who had suffered. During the time I was being questioned, Maria had been picked up by the police several times for questioning. This had been a terrifying experience, and she was wrestling with it. Now, realizing that I intended to continue doing the Lord's work, and that my commitment remained unchanged, she became very angry with me.

During the period of questioning and torture, Maria developed diabetes. We didn't know what was wrong with her, only that she just kept feeling worse and worse. We went to the doctor, who checked her blood sugar and found it to be 400+. He gave her two days before he would begin insulin shots.

Brother Ion began to encourage her when he heard about it. He told her, "God will help you. Do not be afraid. Christians have another Hope."

The people from the church came to our house and we prayed together for her. The Holy Spirit spoke to her. He said, "As a sign that God has heard you, your sugar will test normal when the doctor checks it. If you will fully believe, the sickness will completely leave."

When we returned to the doctor two days later, her blood count had dropped to 130. The doctors considered it a miracle. Doctor Popescu said, "We treat and operate, but only God can heal."

Now that the severe tests were coming, Satan tried to discourage her. I tried to calm her fears by explaining that I wasn't going to do anything for a while because of the physical pain I was in. "Later, when I get well," I told her, "we'll see what the Lord wants me to do." I never really told her that I wouldn't transport Bibles again. I would have quit, but I knew the growing need for Bibles, so I couldn't lie to her. In any case, she calmed down after a while.

By now it was November, 1980. A few days after our conversation, I went fishing on the Siret River. A couple of friends, one from Bihor and another from Bucharest, found me there. They had many Bibles with them. I quickly learned that the two men had gone to our home first.

When Maria opened the door, she appealed to them, "Please... leave our house. We have just come through a great trial a few days ago and we don't want another one."

"Where is your husband?" they asked her.

"Fishing," she told them. "Now, please leave our house. I don't want the police to find you here."

They left, but they came looking for me along the river.

After a while, they located me.

Now, with tears in their eyes, they told me my wife had been afraid to let them in the house. They begged me to allow them to leave the Bibles they had brought. What could I do? I left my fishing and went with them to deliver the Bibles to the Russian border!

After we had fervently prayed, we felt assured the angel of the Lord would go with us all the way. The border was about one hundred miles away. Our journey would have been a rough one if God had not been with us. On our way I told the Brothers not to be hurt by Maria's behavior. "She's just afraid the police will catch me again. I'm followed everywhere by them. Even our next door neighbors have cooperated with the police. We are watched constantly."

When we arrived at our destination, the Prut River, the man who was to pick up the Bibles was there. We simply loaded the Bibles into his car and he was on his way in less than an hour. We were so happy for the miraculous way God had worked. We thanked Him for the prosperous trip and returned home.

It was about 3:30 p.m. when we arrived home. I found my wife still up and crying. When she saw me come through the door, she said, "Dumitru, didn't I tell you not to go transporting Bibles anymore? I can't live this way!"

I didn't have any words of comfort for her. What could I say to her? She wanted me to promise that I wouldn't work with Bibles anymore. I couldn't tell her what she wanted to hear because, deep within my heart, I knew I had to do this work for God. Even after all I had been through, I somehow wanted to serve God more than ever. If I hadn't been stopped by now, nothing could stop me.

I told Maria I would do what was best. "Try not to worry, and please give us some food to eat. Then we can all go to bed." After we ate, I showed the Brothers to their room.

"If you want to continue working with me, Brothers Ioan and Nicu, you are going to have to pray for me and my family. God will have to change my wife because she isn't feeling a bit good about my ministry."

They agreed. Together we went on our knees in prayer, asking God to solve the problem. After I went to bed, I couldn't sleep for worry. But the next morning when Maria awoke, she said, "I don't have any objections to anything that you want to do concerning the work of God. I'll just have to believe that He'll protect you."

I turned to my wife. "Maria, the hand of God is at work, and He works in miraculous ways. I am so thankful for your words."

Not long after, Brothers Ioan and Nicu returned with two men from Holland. As soon as they had entered my home, one of them said, "Let's pray, and see what God has to say." While we were praying, God showed me the wife of one of the men from Holland, laying on a bed, near death. Through prophecy, God spoke, "If your wife will confess her sins when you return home, I will heal her." The man begin to cry and asked for an anointed handkerchief. I anointed one, prayed over it and gave it to him. Early the next morning they left.

Late one night, about 1½-2 months later, I heard a knock at the door. When I opened the door, there were two men and a woman standing there. I invited them in. As soon as they entered, one of the men asked me if I knew who the woman was. When I said, "No.", he said, "This is the woman you prayed for two months ago, by anointed handkerchief. She had a terminal illness. We had given up all hope. But God has healed her!"

God certainly heard our prayers. From April 1980 until

119

June of 1984 I transported Bibles without any trouble and without detainments of any kind.

I never stopped visiting Christians, praying for the sick or helping those who were hungry. We had some problems with the police from time to time, and I would be called to testify. But nothing serious happened.

The authorities checked my house about once a week for Bibles, but the angel of God would tell me when they were coming and I always had time to hide everything before the arrived. My family lived in constant apprehension because of the beatings and tortures I had faced before. But those last four years were easier than the previous ones. On a number of occasions, God kept us form being questioned when we had a car full of Bibles. The police would just tell us to move along. Only God could have kept them from seeing or finding our illegal cargo.

After about fifteen years of distributing Bibles, the missionaries and I decided to figure out how many we had actually moved. **We counted 300,000 Bibles, plus the New Testaments and other literature we had sent into Russia.**

But, about this time, our smuggling system by train collapsed. During one particular train shipment, as the Christians were unloading the box cars in Russia, the Secret Police appeared. The Christians were arrested and immediately imprisoned.

During this same period of time, we were carrying Bibles into Russia by bus, also. On one particular boarder crossing, the guards found the hidden Bibles. Written on one of the packages of Bibles was the complete name and address of a Russian Brother that was to receive some of them. The Russian Secret Police went to the Brother's home and searched it. Finding many Bibles, they arrested him and some other Brothers that were there at the time.

The bus driver was not held because his brother-in-law

was the head customs official at that crossing.

About the same time of this discovery, my daughter, Virginia, gave me money to buy a year's supply of honey in Bucecea. When I arrived in Bucecea, I met the bus driver on the road. He told me he was on his way to my home. After explaining the Bible discovery on his bus, he said he needed to pay the other customs officials to keep them from turning him in, so he could continue to carry Bibles. I gave him all the money I had, including the money Virginia had given me for honey. I also borrowed money from some friends, to make sure he had enough.

After paying the other customs officials, he was able to continue carrying Bibles to Russia for many more years.

On another trip, I stopped in Constanta at the Acustacioae home. This family had known the Lord for a long time. The very second I stepped through the door I heard the phone ring. "It's for you!" I was told.

"Dumitru, it's Vultor. Can you come to my house right away?"

"I'll be there as fast as I can," I answered.

I had to go by bus so I went to the station. It took an hour to get to Brother Vultor's home. "Brother Dumitru, I called you here to pray for my son who is two years old. He cannot walk. He was born with one leg shorter than the other."

"Well, do you believe your son will be healed and able to walk?"

"Yes, we believe with all of our hearts that God will heal our son."

"If you truly believe, then let's get down on our knees and pray, so God will do His work."

After we read some scriptures, we began to pray and God did a miracle with that little child. The right leg began to grow, and within seconds was as long as the other one!

When we finished praying, he was walking without any difficulty at all. One would never have known that he had ever been crippled. How we praised God! After a few days I returned home. I had only been home two days when a telegram came from Botosani - from the Azamfiri family - asking me to come quickly to their home. Their twenty-one year old son was being attacked by a demonic spirit. He was a good, strong man who loved his mother and father, but when under the control of this spirit, he beat his parents. He had written terrible words in black on his bedroom walls. He wouldn't talk or listen to anyone. He was unable to sleep or leave his room and he repeatedly snarled, "There is no God!"

Unafraid, I went into his room without saying a word. I knew it had to be a satanic spirit that was making him conduct himself in such an insane manner. I studied the spirit and then I said, "In the name of Jesus Christ, I order you, spirit of the Devil, to leave this man." Then we went to our knees to pray that the evil spirit would leave him alone. To our great joy, God healed him. As a demonstration of God's healing, the young man removed from his walls all of the vile things he had written there. Weeping, he clung to his mother and father, begging for their forgiveness.

About that same time, an unbelieving woman who lived in our village came down with cancer. Her family was against all forms of religion. But, eventually, she came to the church after she had spent all of her money on doctors who were unable to help her. After exploring every medical avenue, she was still sick.

At the first service she attended, the Holy Spirit spoke through a Christian saying, "If you will decide to follow Me and be My servant, I, the Lord, will give you your health and your pain will go away. I am a powerful God."

The woman was amazed that God had spoken to her. She asked the people to pray for her. We anointed her with oil and asked God to heal her. God did what only HE could do - removed the disease from her body! From that moment on she chose to follow God, and so did her children.

My work among the Romanian people was so rewarding and powerful, it never crossed my mind that I might someday have to leave my homeland. Even though I had prophecies about this - and even though the angel of God appeared once saying that I was chosen to go and preach the word of God in other countries - I wasn't prepared for the REALITY that awaited me.

During another visit from some missionaries, my address fell into the hands of the police. Nothing happened to the men because I wasn't home, but two days later I was called to the police station.

"Look Duduman, we're finished playing around with you. You have some choices. Either you go to prison for the rest of your life, you go to a mental institution or you get out of the country. You are no good for Romania."

I was stunned. "How can I go to another country where I don't know anybody? Everything I've worked for is here. I have a house and everything I need. My relatives are here. My friends are here. How can I leave?"

When the police colonel heard this he said, "I really don't care what you want or don't want. I've given you your choices."

My heart was aching as I went home that day. I told Maria, Virginia and Mike what had been said. We had little time to make plans. Two days later when I was at church a policeman came to me and said, "Mr. Duduman, you are to be at the police station Monday morning at 8:00 a.m.. Report to the passport section."

I went home and told my wife I had been called to the

passport division of the police station. "I don't know what they have in mind," I muttered.

I waited impatiently for morning to come so I could get the police encounter over with. I was there at 8:00 a.m. and was told to wait my turn. Hardly ten minutes passed before I heard my name. A short man appeared with his glasses in his hand. He led me into his office and said, "I am Daigr, the sheriff of this section. I have received orders to get you on your way out of the country. I think you'd be wise not to refuse. You don't want to spend the rest of your life in some jail. And nobody likes being in an insane asylum where just one shot of medication can ruin your mind. You'd better accept this offer to go to America now, before it's too late."

A surge of weakness made my arms and legs feel limp. What would I do in America? I didn't know the language. All my friends would be left behind - family - future - everything! "I will go if my family goes with me; my wife, daughter, son-in-law and grandsons. If you won't let me do this, I won't fill out the application."

"So that you won't think I'm an evil man, I will give you two days to go to Bucharest, to the American Embassy, to let them know the situation you're in. They have to accept you because you have been doing favorable work for a long time transporting Bibles. Even though you say we don't know anything, we do. Go see them. Meanwhile, I'll see what I can do about whether your children can go with you or not."

I took the bus at 1:00 p.m. and was home by 2:00 p.m.. I told Maria the situation, then took the train that night for Bucharest. I arrived there at 5:00 a.m.. I waited for the American Embassy to open at nine.

Considering how intensely the Romanians wanted to make me leave the country, the Americans were very cool, even Vice-Consul Beton and Mr. Maloney. They told me very plainly that I did not have a file, therefore I could not go to America.

"I know I have a file, because my situation came to light after I was violently beaten," I told them.

Nevertheless, with no regret, the Americans told me that they could not help me. At the moment I was glad that the Embassy wanted nothing to do with me. Maybe once the Romanians heard this they wouldn't try to make me leave anymore. Perhaps they would leave me alone and I could live in peace.

I would soon see that my thoughts were not God's thoughts.

When I left the Embassy, I went to visit the family of some of our dearest friends. When I got there I didn't stay long. They invited me to go with them to visit a Christian woman who was a prophetess. God had often used her spiritual gifts to strengthen believers.

We prayed together, then the Holy Spirit spoke through Sister Feraru. "Listen Dumitru, I have decided that your feet will not walk on this ground any longer. In a short time you will go to a foreign land where you have never been. Even if you don't want to, you will be forced to leave. The mouth of the Lord has spoken it."

After this word, I went back home to the passport department. "Leave me alone," I told the officer, "because the American Embassy wouldn't accept me."

"I don't care if the Americans accept you or not! I have received orders from the Internal Ministry to give you your forms to leave this country. Whether you want them or not, I'm giving you those forms today."

He even called the Minister while I was sitting there. "Give them to him," the man barked into the phone. "Just get him out of our hair!"

125

I was pleased to see that I had forms for the whole family, but I was also troubled because I knew how deeply Maria and Virginia dreaded leaving Romania. But having no choice, I took the forms and went home.

All the way home I kept praying, "Please, God, give me the words to convince my wife and daughter that we have to leave Romania whether we want to or not."

In this worried state I arrived at the house. What would I say? I wasn't even in the house yet, when I heard Maria's voice. "Dumitru, what did the police want from you?"

"What can I say, Maria? They gave me forms for leaving the country."

After that, there was silence but for the sound of my wife and daughter crying. Finally, Maria said, "Dumitru, I have worked here all my life with hardships and pain, sometimes hungry with no clothes. At last we were able to build a house and, now when we have everything we want, I can't live here! I'm forced to leave my homeland, and leave just like that!"

I tried to talk to her. "It's okay, Maria," I began. "Please don't cry anymore. Anywhere we go, if we trust in God and serve Him, He will be with us. He will be the One who will protect us anywhere we are. Don't be afraid. Don't be sad, because no matter how we try, we can't change the mind of God. Let's just really trust the Lord. Then we won't have anything to worry about."

All the while I was trying to strengthen myself. For all of us it was a great tragedy. I couldn't eat, for all the joy had left my heart. I tried to think what I would do in a country I had never seen - with people I didn't know. It was useless to even try to imagine.

Time was passing quickly. I filled out the forms and took them to the passport department and, shortly, I received notice that my passports were coming in the mail.

Seeing I had no time to waste, I went to the embassy at Bucharest and, this time, God worked in a miraculous way. To my amazement, I was accepted very graciously by the American Ambassador. The man must have been a believer. He talked so differently than the others.

"Mr. Duduman," he asked gently, "are you a Christian?"

"Yes sir I am."

"Then I will try to do everything I can for you, and even more importantly, you must pray for God's help, too. Go home, and when I call you, come back."

I went home and together with my loved ones, began ten days of fasting and prayer. I said, "God, if you have decided that we should leave Romania, please take care of my case."

In answer to our prayers, a few days later I was called to the Embassy by telegram. I said, "God, this is a sign that You have heard and answered our prayers. Please continue to help me."

The next day I returned to Bucharest by train. At 9:00 a.m., March 24, 1984, I was in the hall of the American Embassy waiting. As I sat in a chair thinking, I heard my name called. A man with a beard led me into his office and asked me to sit down. Then he reached out to shake hands with me. "I am the Vice Consul of the American Embassy. My name is Asalam Alem. Your case and file have a lot of charges against you for transporting Bibles. After you gave Bibles to certain people, they filed declarations. They are there along with your arrest records. This file was made up in 1980 by Mrs. Banciur. Now Mr. Duduman, I want to know what you have done that has caused them to throw you out of the country? Why won't the Romanian government allow you to live here?"

I then explained as best I could about the Bibles, about

my faith and about the healings that God had performed in answer to my prayers. As I explained about the healings, tears began to pour down the Vice-Consul's face.

"Mr. Duduman," he explained, "I am crying because my wife is suffering with a very rare blood disease. I've spent all kinds of money on doctors, but no one has found a cure. My last hope is that God will heal her. And I believe God brought you here so I could talk to you. Perhaps through you, my wife can be healed."

I nodded. "If you will believe with all of your heart and trust God fully, my friends and I will pray for her at exactly 9:00 p.m. tonight."

That night, I went to a Christian meeting. Although I wasn't sure they would be getting together that night, I asked God to let them be there. They were. After I explained about the Vice-Consul's wife, we began to pray. We had hardly begun when an old woman I didn't know spoke out. "Listen, my son, you came here with a burden. I have heard your prayers and will work in a way you cannot imagine. In a short time you will go to a land that you have never seen and I will fill you with My Spirit. Through you, many will be healed. I will wake up many others through your words. The mouth of the Lord has spoken it!"

I could hardly sleep that night, I was so excited to see what would happen when I went to the Embassy. I was sure God had healed the man's wife, and I wanted to see what her husband was going to say.

At 9:00 a.m., sharp, I was at the Embassy and the man was waiting for me, full of joy. He wept as he told me, "Last night at 9:00 p.m. I prayed with my wife just as you told me. This morning when they checked her blood, I thought the doctor would never come out. When he finally appeared his face was beaming. 'Some sort of miracle has happened

128

to your wife,' he said. 'Her blood cells are normal.' I thanked God immediately! He has changed our lives forever!"

While he was talking, I was thanking God silently that He had given me favor with the American Embassy.

"Don't worry that you won't be accepted in America," He told me, "because America needs people like you. With God's help you will be able to achieve anything you want. You will not have to waste your time coming back to the Embassy. When we're ready, we'll call you. So that the Romanian government won't bother you, I'll call the Internal Ministry and tell them the situation will be taken care of soon."

I shook hands with him and left with but one thought in my heart. God knows how to give victory to His people. As long as I have the Lord on my side, I don't have to worry.

I prayed silently as I made my way home, "Once again, I see, God, that all things are done according to Your will. And no matter how bad things seem to be, You still give the victory!"

THE BEAUTIFUL ROMANIAN COUNTRYSIDE I MUST NOW LEAVE

HEADING HOME AFTER A DAY'S WORK IN THE FIELDS

Chapter Nine

A JOURNEY INTO THE UNKNOWN

We tried to be about our Father's business as we waited for our passports. On a number of occasions His messenger appeared to me and gave me advice, preparing me for the future. One day as I was sitting on my bed, I saw a man in white clothes. He had a trumpet in his hand. As I watched he blew it three times. "Wake up!" he announced. "The day is coming!"

I was on my feet in seconds sharing my vision with Maria.

Later, I fell asleep on the sofa. The same man appeared to me in a dream. "I'm telling you to wake up because the time of your departure is drawing near. In 121 days, at 10:00 a.m., you will leave this country. Tomorrow you will receive a telegram that will gladden your heart!"

I told the dream to my family and we counted up the days. According to the angel we would leave Romania on July 24, 1984, at 10:00 a.m..

I waited impatiently for the promised telegram. When the postman brought it, it was from the American Embassy. I signed for it and read it excitedly. It instructed my family to go to the Embassy in ten days, just as the angel had promised.

In just a short time Mike, my son-in-law rushed in from work. "Father!" Mike burst out excitedly, "the passports came last week! We need to pick them up!"

This news surprised me. It was so unexpected. I thanked God for working in such a miraculous way. The next day the family planned to pick them up.

As requested, we arrived at the Embassy. What date would they place on our visas? My heart pounded with anticipation. When the officer stamped the visa inside my passport he said as clearly as could be, "You will be leaving this country on July 24th."

His words filled our ears like an explosion. We felt like screaming for joy. Even though we didn't want to leave our homeland and we didn't know where we were going or what we were going to do, we rejoiced in the power of God's faithful word to us. We all agreed that we were not afraid of anything as long as God was with us.

As soon as we arrived home, we began to put our home in order for moving. We had a mink farm, which worried us the most. To sell hundreds of minks in four months would take a miracle. In spite of our concern, buyers came from all over, not only purchasing them at higher prices than we expected, but they also brought gifts.

As the time of our departure drew closer, friends and loved ones started coming to visit us saying sad goodbyes. This time was difficult for us. We all wept. It was impossible not to. As I write this, the tears still burn my eyes and my heart aches.

Every day my house was full of visitors. Day after day I found myself unable to answer the one question everyone persistently asked, "Why does it have to be like this?"

The time went so fast. I wished I could have made it longer. Neither I nor my family could stop crying. Meanwhile the police were following me everywhere, watching everything I did. It seemed like they felt sorry about letting me go.

One week before I was to leave, at about 8:00 p.m., four policeman appeared at my door. "We just came by to see how you're feeling," one of them said. They struck me on the head and back with their blackjacks, then laughed in ridicule and left. Horrified that they would dare to do something so cruel and inhuman, we could only keep our mouths shut and hold our tempers.

Only five days before we left another incident saddened me. We had a dog named Labus, a big strong, white animal with black spots. He was a handsome dog who always barked out a welcome when I came home. Even when I was far away he somehow knew I was coming. In the winter we would tie him to a sled and he'd pull my grandsons on the ice. Now when we were getting ready to leave, he wouldn't bark. He wouldn't eat. He grew more and more depressed. The boys tried to play with him, but he wouldn't play. He became more withdrawn with every passing day. How could he know we were leaving?

On July 13th we were all standing outside. Labus looked around at all of us, barked three times and ran away. The next morning we found him dead on the river bank. Even an animal shared the agony of our coming separation.

In the following four days, we visited all the places we loved. We walked together through forests with their thick woods, tall grasses and thousands of flowers that filled the spring air with wonderful fragrances and colors. We wandered through places where we once picked mushrooms, ate wild berries, and drank ice cold water from bubbling springs. We made private pilgrimages to favorite havens where we once had been free to sit and think, listening to the gentle, delicate songs of birds and watching bees flit from one flower to another.

133

My grandsons had taken some of their first steps here and later learned to run - joyfully trying to catch butterflies. Even the bushes on the banks of the Siret would never be forgotten - or the river's current with its continuous surging rhythm. All our lives we had enjoyed the pleasures of diving in for refreshing swims, or lowering our nets into the water to catch a platter full of fish for dinner. Each of these things is etched in my mind. Even now it almost seems that I am there.

Two days before we left, we prepared a hugh feast and a large group of our neighbors, relatives and friends came. We were the only family that had ever left that village. We could hardly make any progress on our packing with so many people coming and going. I gave away everything we had worked so hard for. The house was taken away by the government. (Later my brother would buy it back from the government for himself). The remaining minks were given to a Christian friend who wanted them. The furniture was given away. Everything was gone! A whole life was gone in one day!

On Monday, the 18th of July, at 8:00 a.m., two cars pulled up in front of the house to take us to the airport. I took our few suitcases and put them in the cars. By 9:00 a.m. I could hardly get our hand baggage out of the house for all the people. We got dressed and tried to eat something, but our appetites were gone. Everybody was crying. At 10:00 a.m. we all got on our knees and prayed one last time together. Outside, I shook hands with over a hundred people - some I will never see again. My heart ached unbelievable. Although I was crying, I tried not to burden everyone with the grief I felt.

It seems but yesterday. Our friends hugged us, saying, "After you go, it will be as though the seven of you have died, but still we will not stop praying and fasting for you to return." The men drove the cars out of the driveway. In just a few minutes we had to go. With tears in our eyes we were looking in all directions. Physically I felt no strength. To this day I don't know any pain more unbearable than leaving your loved ones, not knowing if you will ever see them again. I looked up to see my oldest grandson running back to kiss the door of the house. Everyone wept uncontrollable. Finally, all we heard was the sound of the automobile engines. We watched the hands of loving friends waving goodbye.

All the way to Bucharest we thought of the good times we'd had there and we cried all the more. I quite often think of the places in Romania and wonder if I will ever lay eyes on them again. Then and now, I can only say, "I will leave everything in the hands of God." On the way to Bucharest we went through the city of Suceava where my son-in-law worked in a glass factory. We stopped long enough for him to tell his fellow workers and friends goodbye. He had worked there ten years. Although the police sometimes made a point of following him, he was loved by his fellow workers.

Mike, too had experienced many difficulties because of his Christian faith. He had been trained to be the head of a corporation but because of his religious beliefs it was very hard for him to obtain even his position as top glass blower. He loved his art of glass blowing and looked forward to practicing it in the United States. There he would not be put down for his religion.

As of today, his wish has not come true. He has been unable to find employment in his line of work here. He continues to ask God to provide him with a quality job in glass blowing, and I believe that he will one day find a way to use the unique skill he worked so hard to learn and love so well.

Arriving at Bucharest, we spent a few more days at the homes of other friends while the police checked our baggage, got our tickets and took care of other small details. Uncertain thoughts raced through my mind. "Whose house am I going to there? Will we find new friends? How will we support ourselves?"

The night before our flight we shared one more prayer and our friends and family members agreed to see us off at the airport. None of us could sleep, so we were up and dressed early. After a word of prayer, we took the luggage out of the house.

At the airport there were about fifty people waiting to tell us goodbye for the last time. After our final farewells, it was announced that everyone with tickets to Italy should board the plane immediately. We shook hands, hugged everyone and made our way down a large hallway. Our luggage was thoroughly checked. My daughter requested that the airport agents not take anything out of her bag. Instead they took her into another room and made her strip to be inspected. They have very ugly methods of searching and we were treated brutally even as we left the country. By the time they finished with us, our entire family was left with only three suitcases! The rest - mostly personal momentos and photographs - was confiscated by the airport agents as a final act of cruelty.

We boarded the plane at 10:00 a.m.. It was the 24th of July. We were on our way.

Our time in Rome provided an interesting transition from Romania to the free world. How strange to see the happiness of the Italian people! In Romania everyone seems depressed and joyless. Romania is one of the poorest countries in the world today. In Rome there were the Italians with their good foods, fruits, vegetables and colorful clothing. Most of all they were free!

During our nine days there we saw many of the sights that make Rome so famous. As we looked around I thought of all the Christians who had given their lives for the Lord in that historic city. I consoled myself thinking that they had suffered far more than I had. They lost everything, including their right to live. I too had sacrificed my possessions, but I had God to thank for the fact that I was alive, and so was my beloved family.

One day the woman at the hotel desk called me aside. "Mr Duduman, you be careful. Someone was just here asking of your whereabouts." Our family had planned to go out for the afternoon, but instead we stayed close to the hotel. Later on I went to the American Embassy. There stood a Romanian woman who had worked in the American Embassy in Bucharest. I had already been informed that she was a spy for the Romanian government. Had she been sent to Rome to assassinate me?

At long last we were on our way to America. Again whirlwinds of thought spun around in our minds. What if no one was waiting for us? Where would we go? What would we do?

My little grandsons sat quietly, safely strapped into the airplane's seats. With very pale and sad faces they asked, "Grandpa, where are we going?"

"I don't know. I wish I did. But I can promise you that God will take care of us."

We arrived in New York on August 3rd. There, we were put in a hotel for one night. I had the telephone numbers of some Christian believers there. Hopefully, I dialed one of them whose name is John Hotea. He was delighted to hear my voice and even happier when I told him where I was. Soon he arrived and we were so encouraged by a time of prayer with him and two other Christians who arrived the next morning.

137

After New York, we finally found our way to Fullerton, California. Our arrival there was a rude awakening. Some strangers greeted us and took us to an apartment they had rented for us. Despite their wonderful intentions, we were deeply troubled, for the smell in the apartment was so terrible that we could hardly bear it. To our amazement the apartments in California allowed dogs and cats that left a vile smell behind, but they didn't want children.

The people who picked us up prepared a wonderful meal for us, but, grateful as we were, we simply couldn't eat. The smell, the dirty walls, and the lack of any place to sleep depressed us. Late into the night we lay on the filthy carpet, weeping.

Great discouragement gripped my wife and children. "If we had not started traveling with Bibles," Maria sobbed, "we would be in our country with our friends and family. We had good things around us."

I stretched out on the floor that night with grave despair in my heart. Both Maria and I were crying. When I eventually fell asleep, I had a strange and remarkable dream.

I found myself back in Romania. Maria and I were there visiting an apple orchard. For some reason we weren't allowed to go in. The owner approached us and said, "What are you doing here? Don't you know that you have no right to be here? Your rights are in America. Get out or I'll call the police!"

I pleaded with the owner to let us walk through the beautiful orchard just one last time, but he would not. As I stood waiting, I suddenly realized that it was getting dark outside, a strange occurrence since it was only about 1:00 p.m.. I looked all around to see where the darkness was coming from and was terrified to see a volcano erupting. Its lava spread over the nearby homes, then began to rise across the ground. "Maria," I said in the dream, "I guess you know we're going to die."

Maria smiled. "I am so happy that I am going to die on Romanian ground."

Then suddenly, an American helicopter lowered to rescue us. When I got inside the copter, I looked into the familiar eyes of the pilot. He was the man dressed in white; the angel of the Lord.

He said nothing, just motioned for us to sit down. When we were high over the ground, he finally spoke, "Look Down." I looked - and the land of Romania was covered with an army of tanks, machine guns, and aircraft, all poised for battle.

"See, all of this evil will eventually happen. This is why the Lord has taken you from Romania, to save you. Now you are in a position to help your people from your new home. You will provide tremendous assistance to your Christian Brothers and Sisters as well as to your loved ones. This is why I have sent you to America. So be strong and trust the Lord fully. He will not let you down."

Next, it seemed we were over California. The angel said, "There is San Francisco. There is Sacramento and Modesto. Soon we will see Los Angeles."

I had no idea there were such places in California, or even in the world. But I still remember the exact names. At last we were over Fullerton where we now live. "You can go home," the angel said, "but I want to tell you what will happen. You have seen a number of cities. The day will come when I will punish the citizens of those cities because of their sins. Their sin has reached into heaven. God will punish them just as he punished Sodom and Gomorrah."

"How will this happen? Surely they are able to defend themselves against any imaginable invasion."

"That is your opinion, not the mind of God. The

139

Russian government will have all the information regarding the whereabouts of American missiles. They will have the exact locations of the weapons factories. Even now they are preparing an attack against America. When America believes there is peace and safety, the Russians will lead an all out attack. They already have it planned! They plan to attack from such remote bases as Cuba, Nicaragua, Central America, Mexico and the ocean. They have had these plans for a long time, but God has not yet allowed them to be fulfilled. Nevertheless, the day will come when America will be punished for her sins by fire."

I was terrified. "Why did you bring me here to die? Why didn't you let me die where my parents died?"

"Don't be afraid." He spoke calmly and quietly. "The pure of heart will not be punished. Those who are untouched by the sins of others, and are faithful and true, will hear the trumpet of God and the voice of God's angel crying, 'Wake up!' They will be told where to go."

"Where will they go?"

The helicopter soared again. I caught my breath, for as I looked down my eyes swept across beautiful cities. Two rivers flowed through one of them and growing alongside the other was a vast, lush forest. "This is your refuge when the times of tribulation fall upon California. Your family, and all those who hear the voice of the Lord, will understand the message of God's mighty trumpet."

Deeply troubled, I awoke from my restless sleep. The next morning I told my family the dream and began fasting for 21 days.

"If the dream is from You, Lord, I pray that I will have it again."

Chapter Ten

HOPE FOR TOMORROW

Even after that powerful revelation, our difficulties persisted. However, three days after I began my fast, I was asked to call on a family where both wife and husband were sick. I prayed for them and they were healed. This encouraged me somewhat.

I finished my fast, but continued to be sickened by the conditions we were in. My family was unhappy and Maria was crying all the time. The apartment was terrible, and we still had no furniture.

Maria suggested I try to find a better place for us to live. I went out and tried hard to find another place. Each time I found a place they would ask if I had children. When I said we had children, they would say, "We don't rent to people with children."

I could not understand this. I thought, "What kind of people are these? They keep dogs in their house but not children!" We were very discouraged.

Late one night I could not sleep. The children were sleeping on the luggage. My wife and daughter were crying. I went outside and walked around. I didn't want them to see me cry. I walked around the building, crying and saying, "God! Why did you punish me? Why did you bring me into

141

this country? I can't understand anybody. If I try to ask anybody anything, all I hear is, 'I don't know.'"

I stopped in front of the apartment and sat on a large rock. Suddenly a bright light came toward me. I jumped to my feet because it looked as if a car was coming directly at me, attempting to run me down! I thought the Romanian Secret Police had tracked me to America, and now they were trying to kill me. But it wasn't a car at all. As the light approached, it surrounded me. From the light I heard the same voice that I had heard so many times in prison. He said, "Dumitru, why are you so despaired?"

I said, "Why did you punish me? Why did you bring me to this country? I have nowhere to lay my head down. I can't understand anybody."

He said, "Dumitru, didn't I tell you I am here with you also? I brought you to this country because this country will burn."

I said, "Then why did you bring me here to burn? Why didn't you let me die in my own country? You should have let me die in jail in Romania!"

He said, "Dumitru, have patience so I can tell you. Get on this." I got on something next to him. I don't know what it was. I also know that I was not asleep. It was not a dream. It was not a vision. I was awake just as I am now. He showed me all of **California** and said, *"This is sodom and Gomorrah! All of this, in one day it will burn!* It's sin has reached the Holy One." Then he took me to **Las Vegas**. *"This is Sodom and Gomorrah. In one day it will burn."* Then he showed me the state of **New York**. "Do you know what this is?" he asked.

I said, "No."

He said, "This is **New York**. *This is Sodom and Gomorrah! In one day it will burn."*

Then he showed me all of **Florida**. "This is **Florida**," he said. *"This is Sodom and Gomorrah! In one day it will burn."*

Then he took me back home to the rock where we had begun. *"All of this I have shown you - IN ONE DAY IT WILL BURN!"*

I said, "How will it burn?"

He said, "Remember what I am telling you, because you will go on television, on the radio and in churches. You must yell with a loud voice. Do not be afraid, because I will be with you."

I said, "How will I be able to go? Who knows me here in America? I don't know anybody here."

He said, "Don't worry yourself. I will go before you. I will do a lot of healing in the American churches, and I will open the doors for you. But do not say anything else besides what I tell you. This country will burn!"

I said, "What will you do with the Church?"

He said, "I want to save the Church, but the churches have forsaken me."

I said, "How did they forsake you?"

He said, "The people praise themselves. The honor that the people are supposed to give Jesus Christ, they take upon themselves. In the churches there are divorces. There is adultery in the churches. There are homosexuals in the churches. There is abortion in the churches; and all other sins that are possible. Because of the sin, I have left some of the churches. You must yell in a loud voice that they must put an end to their sinning. **They must turn toward the Lord.** The Lord never gets tired of forgiving. They must draw close to the Lord, and live a clean live. If they have sinned until now, they must put an end to it, and start a new life as the Bible tells them to live."

I said, "How will America burn? America is the most powerful country in this world. Why did you bring us here to burn? Why didn't you at least let us die where ALL the Dudumans have died?"

He said, "Remember this, Dumitru. The Russian spies have discovered where the nuclear warehouses are in America. When the Americans will think that it is peace and safety - from the middle of the country, some of the people will start fighting against the government. The government will be busy with internal problems. Then from the ocean, from Cuba, Nicaragua, Mexico,..." (He told me two other countries, but I didn't remember what they were.) "...they will bomb the nuclear warehouses. When they explode, America will burn!"

"What will you do with the Church of the Lord? How will you save the ones that will turn toward you?" I asked.

He said, "Tell them this: **how I saved the three young ones from the furnace of fire, and how I saved Daniel in the lions den, is the same way I will save them.**"

The angel of the Lord also told me, "I have blessed this country because of the Jewish people who are in this country. I have seven million Jews in this country, but they do not want to recognize the Lord. They didn't want to thank God for the blessings they received in this country."

"Israel doesn't want to recognize Jesus Christ. They put their faith in the Jewish people in America. But, when America burns, the Lord will raise China, Japan and other nations to go against the Russians. They will beat the Russians and push them all the way to the gates of Paris. Over there they will make a treaty, and appoint the Russians as their leaders. They will then unite against Israel."

"When Israel realizes she does not have the strength of America behind her, she will be frightened.That's when she will turn to the Messiah for deliverance. That's when the Messiah will come. Then, the church will meet Jesus in the air, and He will bring them back with Him to the Mount of

Olives. At that time the battle of Armageddon will be fought."

When I heard all of this I said, "If you are truly the angel of the Lord, and everything you have told me is true, then all you have said must be written in the Bible."

He said, "Tell everyone to read from **Jeremiah 51:8-15, Revelation chapter 18,** and **Zechariah chapter 14,** where Christ fights against those who possess the earth. After His victory," the angel said, "there will be one flock and one Shepherd. There will be no need for light. The Lamb of God will be the Light. There will be no sickness, no tears, and no deaths. There will only be eternal joy and God will be the ruler. There will be only one language. Only one song. And no need for a translator!"

"And, Dumitru," he continued, "a word of warning. If you keep anything from the American people that you are told, I will punish you severely."

"How will I know that this is for real - that it will really happen?" I asked.

"As a sign that I have spoken to you, tomorrow before you wake I will send someone to bring you a bed, and at noon I will send you a car and a bucket of honey. After which, I will send someone to pay your rent."

The angel left. My prayer had been answered. The dream had been repeated in a more powerful way through a real live revelation. Now I awaited it's confirmation.

I went into the house and fell into a sound sleep, but was up early in the morning. Excitement surged through me because I wanted to see if the angel had spoken the truth. Sure enough, that very morning a Christian man knocked on our apartment door before I was awake. "I've brought you a bed," he said. "I dreamed last night that you had no bed to sleep on."

With tears in my eyes I thanked him and he went his

way. Before long, a family came to visit. The son looked at me kindly and said, "Brother Duduman, God told me last night in a dream that you need a car. We have two cars and God said to give you one. I also brought you a bucket of honey - in His name!"

The next day they brought over the car. It was a 1968 Chevrolet, and it ran very well. He said, "I've been using it until now. I don't know when I'll get another one, but some Romanian Christians gave me this one. So I want to return the favor and give it to you."

Well, the only thing left was the rent. How was God going to work that out?

Over the years I had received countless Bibles from a men named Brother Wurmbrandt, but I'd never known where he lived. Now, God was about to meet another of my needs through this kind man.

A Christian friend came to me and said, "Brother Duduman, come with me and meet Brother Wurmbrandt. He'd love to see you and visit with you." Of course, I went with him.

It was a great pleasure to visit Brother Wurmbrandt's home. Together we shared stories of God's grace, and the wonders He had worked as Bibles were delivered to His people. When it came time to leave, we prayed. Then God put it on Brother Wurmbrandt's heart to give me $500.

The promised rent money! How wonderfully God worked that day! I thanked him with tears in my eyes. After returning home, I gathered my family around. We knelt before the Lord, thanking Him for His goodness. Then I went to the manager and paid my debt.

Life was very hard those first months in America. In Italy we had been asked, "To whom are you going in America? Who do you know? What do you have there?"

I always replied, "I have my Lord Jesus Christ, and He

will take care of me." And in spite of all the hardships, I felt His powerful hand again and again.

We were very sad because bills were coming and there was no money with which to pay them. Then a miraculous thing happened. Brother Harlan Popov, the founder of "*Door of Hope*", who had once sent a large shipment of Bibles to me in Romania, learned I was in America. His son came to our apartment along with some other young people. They took many pictures and shared our situation with Brother Popov. Brother Popov invited me to travel with him to share my experiences in Romania. I traveled with him for about a year, for which he paid me $300 a month. With God's help, I was able to send some money to Romania to help those who had less than I.

One Sunday, in a church service, God used me to deliver a prophetic word to a Romanian woman -- if she and her family did not repent of their sins and turn to God, a "flag of mourning" would be put over their home.

A few days later I learned that she had been killed in a car accident, leaving four children. When I heard this, my heart ached. I was used to helping people, and now all I had was twenty dollars. Nevertheless, I needed to do something for that poor family. I couldn't find anyone who could change the twenty, so finally I put the whole thing in the collection plate. "God will help me if I help someone else," I promised myself.

When I got home, I told Maria that I had given away all the money. "I'm not sorry that you gave it," she said, "but what are we going to use to buy milk and bread for the children?"

"Maria," I answered quietly, "God has always taken care of us. He always will."

The next day a Brother knocked on our door. When I answered the door, he held out $50.00 and said, "Here,

God told me to give this to you."

Later that day some other believers came, bringing detergent, spoons, pots, pans, plates and food.

By now I had learned about Goodwill stores. There, I was able to purchase a bed, a sofa and a few other necessities. But still the bills continued to come in. I didn't have enough to pay them and I could find no way to shake them off.

Mike and Virginia struggled with the idea of finding work. "If only one of us could get a job. We still need so many things," they said.

One day a christian man asked, "How are you getting along financially, Dumitru?"

"It's been very hard," I answered quite honestly.

"I know it's very hard at the start. I've been there, too. Let me give you some advice. Collect papers and tin cans, turn them in to the recycling center and you will be able to earn a little money that way."

That's exactly what we did. The very next day, Michael, Virginia and I started collecting newspapers and tin cans. That was the first money we earned in America. A short time later, the Lord led me to borrow some money.

Some time later, I received a letter from a pastor in Missouri, requesting prayer for cancer. I sent a handkerchief that I had anointed and prayed over. I asked the pastor to place it across his forehead, praying, and God would heal him.

He did as I suggested, and God DID heal him. He quickly wrote me a letter, requesting that I come to share my testimony within one month. He said he would pay my fare.

After a period of time, I found a translator and bought two plane tickets. We flew to Missouri.

While I was in Missouri, I received a phone call from a

woman in Indiana. She asked to speak to me. While I was speaking to her, God showed me she could not walk. She said, "How did you know? I haven't told anyone." I said, "God showed me."

"The Lord promised me I would be healed if you came and prayed for me," she said. "I believe that somehow you will come."

I didn't give her an answer at that time. When I hung up the telephone, I prayed, "God, if you really want this woman to be healed, send me a car so I can get there."

Satan arrived first, bringing disbelief into my heart. But later that night, at a Christian church, the pastor told the people that I needed to get to Indiana, but didn't have a car. Everyone was surprised when a young man got up and spoke out. "I will loan my car, and you can drive it to Indiana." The most amazing aspect of his generous act was that he had just bought the car a week before.

He grinned at our shocked faces. "A neighbor can take me to work while Brother Duduman is in Indiana."

The next day we left for Indiana. When we had arrived and met the woman, she told us that Dieg from Open Doors had come by her home and told her to call me and ask me to pray for her. She said she had been in a car accident four years earlier and had been paralysed ever since. We prayed for the woman and she was healed. The woman later went on national television and gave her testimony.

And through her, God opened another door in Indiana. I was invited to appear on a television broadcast with Brother Lester Sumerall. That was the real beginning of my ministry in America.

After that inspiring journey, we returned the car to the gracious Brother in Missouri. We gratefully thanked him. We also learned that God had worked in such a way that our air fare back to California was paid by the church.

Soon God did another great miracle. Only a short time after I returned to Fullerton, a man called me about his wife, Lenuta. She was thirty years old. She had been paralyzed by a spinal injection given to her during childbirth. Even before her baby's delivery, she'd had severe headaches for years. Virginia and I went to their home to pray for her. I anointed her with oil and we prayed for her. God then gave me a prophecy for her. He said He had healed her, and she should believe with all her heart. As soon as we had finished praying, she got up, served us food and drinks, then started cleaning the house to see what she was able to do. She was completely healed!

A short time later, I received an invitation to return to Indiana and speak in some churches there.

What a great difference there is between communism and capitalism! Here in America, a Christian is free to come and go as he pleases. He is honored. By way of contrast, in a communist country, Christians are oppressed and very limited in what they are allowed to do. We have great reason to thank God for the liberty in which we live.

After those first trips to Indiana, several missionary Brothers came to see me. Brother Dan Wooding was a joy to meet. It is because of his suggestion that I have written this book.

Brother Bernard from Holland also visited me. He had come to my home a few times in Romania. "Can't you stay longer?" I asked him. "It would be a joy to have you."

He laughed out loud. "In Romania you would have said, 'go quickly', but here you ask me to stay longer!"

It was also a great joy to again meet Brother Andrew. How I appreciate people like him who have given their lives by stretching out willing hands to take God's Word to those in need. Many have suffered much for this work.

I now travel throughout the US preaching God's message and praying for the sick, as I have been appointed by God, and because of my love for the American people. It is not an easy message to preach but God encourages me. I am doing it as long as He wants me too. I have traveled a lot and can tell that more and more people are hearing the message. I pray that all will repent and that God may have mercy on them. I'm in God's hands and give Him credit for using me in His work. Throughout the years I have continued to receive messages from God. Through this my faith grows and I receive more courage to work for Him.

With great joy and hope we are working toward the time when His Word will be completely fulfilled throughout the world.

With God's help, my family and I have committed ourselves to joyfully serve Him here. We will continue preaching, praying, healing the sick, feeding the hungry and doing the works of Jesus until He comes to take us home.

LIFE IN ROMANIA GOES ON...

...BUT AT A SLOWER PACE

152

Chapter Eleven

A HAND OF HELP

Beginning a mission work to help the the poor Romanians (see chapter 12 - "Return to Romania" - January, 1990), was not something I had ever thought of. When we received our first direction from God in January, 1985, we had only been in the United states less than four months! We could not speak english, we had no money, we knew no one, and we had no idea WHAT a mission was, much less how to operate one!. BUT GOD SAID, "Start a mission. I will be with you. I will send people to help you as you need them."

Each thing we needed to do, God would reavel to us. I would be sleeping, and God would show me in a dream to go to a certain place and someone would help me with filling out papers we needed. I would have a vision showing or telling me about another step that needed to be done. A prophetic word would come, with specific directions in yet another item that needed completed for the mission. God was very explicit on each thing that needed to be done to establish the mission. God told us specific names, places, etc.

No matter what the cost, or whether we understood or agreed, we would obey God in EVERY detail He told us to do or say. I am sure that is why the mission work has grown so fast. God has blessed it because of obedience to His word!

Over the years God has fulfilled His promise to be with us, and help us in every detail of His work through us. Without God's help, we would have never been able to begin the *Hand of Help* mission.

1989

Today I look back upon the years I spent in Communism. Every day I more clearly understand God's purpose in sending me to America. I consider the things I have suffered to be much less painful than what is being endured by those who continue to live under the shadow of Communism and the madness of Nicolae Ceausescu. How could the Romanian people be happy about anything?

On behalf of the people in Romania; Maria, Mike, Virginia, our three grandsons, and I have begun our own little ministry, *Hand of Help*. We are working diligently to send as many supplies as possible back to the needy Christians in Romania. We buy, package and ship - coffee, meat, canned goods and other provisions they cannot purchase for themselves. In the process we have made new friends, received a new vision and are learning a new way of life.

It wasn't easy, but with God's help we lived through all the hard times. I am stirred when I think back and remember that I didn't know how to run a ministry or speak English; and that I borrowed the money to start the ministry. Still, I did everything through God's guidance. I am overjoyed that I obeyed, because everything has become a great blessing for the ones in need. God told me, "I'll give you people and send you help, but all at it's appointed time." It has happened. God is keeping His promises toward His people. By having God on our side and believing in Him, everything will go according to His plan and we will come through victorious. Praying and fasting has helped my strength to grow.

1990

One day in 1989 a man dressed in white appeared to me and said, "Prepare. You will be going to Romania with Bibles in a short time. Things will change there." Just imagine, for more than five years I *knew* there would never be a chance for me to go to Romania again. Now God's messenger was telling me I would be going back - with Bibles! It wasn't easy, but still I obeyed, and told others about it, also. Four months later, the same person appeared to me again. "I came to tell you that Ceausescu is going to be executed in three weeks." After telling my family and friends, we began to count down the days. It happened, just as he said. We may never understand the way God works.

In April 1990 I took my first trip there. I was filled with joy, but I also shed many tears. It was wonderful to freely be able to bring Bibles into the same country where I had been tortured for smuggling them.

It was on that trip that I understood the importance of the help I had been sending for the three previous years. Many came to me then, saying if I hadn't helped them they might have been dead by now. On my way back to the States from the short trip, about three hours into the flight, my heart began to ache. To show me that He had sent me, God sent me a sign which strengthened me greatly. While coming back from Romania I was given this vision: As I was sitting in the seat, a white bird with a golden and shiney beak appeared. In it's beak it had a letter which it opened with it's feet and a voice said, "Read."

So, I began to read. The letter said, "I was with you in Romania and I am with you now while you return. Because you were not partial and you gave to everybody....because you obeyed and did as I told you to do...my blessings will be over you even more than they have been. Do everything that I put in your heart to do, and I the Lord will help you. I will open the doors which were not opened until now, and I will bless you so you can work for Me. I am with you." Then the bird closed the letter, and waving good-bye with it's wing, disappeared. I was restrengthened and I said, "I trust in You fully. Oh, Lord, You work as You wish."

I got home safely. The next day I received a letter inviting me to a television program called *God's News Behind the News*.

My work DID get harder and it gradually split into two parts. One part of it is traveling throughout the United States preaching, praying for the sick and leading people to God. The other part is ministering to the people of Romania through money, food, clothing and Bibles. Because of the new freedom for Christians in Romania, many people are now coming to God. A need has risen to build new churches. The volume of people has outgrown the few churches that were there. We are providing the finances to build them wherever they are unable to do it themselves. Our newest project is building an orphanage in the city of Botosani. At this time there is NO place for children over 6 years old in this area of Romania.

SECOND EDITION UPDATE

1991

In the days of Ceausescu, *Hand of Help* sent countless numbers of food packages to the poor. Many families would not have survived without this assistance. *Hand of Help* also sponsored more than 300 families out of the refugee camps in the countries surrounding Romania, and brought them to America.

Since the revolution in Romania, *Hand of Help* has been able to establish a government-recognized branch in the country. This enables *Hand of Help* to better continue meeting the needs of the people. *Hand of Help* continues to ship food and clothing, as well as Bibles. *Hand of Help* has built several churches and assisted many others with funds to build, rebuild or expand. *Hand of Help* has also held crusades to reach those who are hungry to hear about God.

In the city of Botosani, there are many orphans. The government provides two orphanages. One takes little ones up to age 3. The other takes children ages 3 to 5. There has been no regular provision after age 6. Many children have ended up in very undesirable places. Some have been sent to homes for the handicapped, and others have ended up in retirement homes. In response to this need, *Hand of Help* decided to build an orphanage that will take children ages 6 to 18. The ground breaking ceremony was held in June 1991. With God's help, the projected target date for opening is 1993. The orphanage will not only provide for the physical care of the children, but will educate them and teach them the love of Jesus as well. Reaching out our *Hand of Help*, we will do everything we can to make the children feel like "family".

FOR FURTHER INFORMATION ABOUT THE
MINISTRY, CONTACT DUMITRU DUDUMAN
THROUGH:

HAND OF HELP, INC.
P.O. BOX 3494
FULLERTON, CALIFORNIA 92634

(714) 447-1313

Chapter Twelve

MESSAGES FROM GOD

AMERICA WILL BURN

September 1984

Late one night I could not sleep. The children were sleeping on the luggage. My wife and daughter were crying. I went outside and walked around. I didn't want them to see me cry. I walked around the building, crying and saying, "God! Why did you punish me? Why did you bring me into this country? I can't understand anybody. If I try to ask anybody anything, all I hear is, 'I don't know.'"

I stopped in front of the apartment and sat on a large rock. Suddenly a bright light came toward me. I jumped to my feet because it looked as if a car was coming directly at me, attempting to run me down! I thought the Romanian Secret Police had tracked me to America, and now they were trying to kill me. But it wasn't a car at all. As the light approached, it surrounded me. From the light I heard the same voice that I had heard so many times in prison. He said, "Dumitru, why are you so despaired?"

I said, "Why did you punish me? Why did you bring me to this country? I have nowhere to lay my head down. I

159

can't understand anybody."

He said, "Dumitru, didn't I tell you I am here with you also? I brought you to this country because this country will burn."

I said, "Then why did you bring me here to burn? Why didn't you let me die in my own country? You should have let me die in jail in Romania!"

He said, "Dumitru, have patience so I can tell you. Get on this." I got on something next to him. I don't know what it was. I also know that I was not asleep. It was not a dream. It was not a vision. I was awake just as I am now. He showed me all of **California** and said, *"This is Sodom and Gomorrah! All of this, in one day it will burn!* It's sin has reached the Holy One." Then he took me to **Las Vegas**. *"This is Sodom and Gomorrah. In one day it will burn."* Then he showed me the state of **New York**. "Do you know what this is?" he asked.

I said, "No."

He said, "This is **New York**. *This is Sodom and Gomorrah! In one day it will burn."*

Then he showed me all of **Florida**. "This is **Florida**," he said. *"This is Sodom and Gomorrah! In one day it will burn."*

Then he took me back home to the rock where we had begun. ***"All of this I have shown you - IN ONE DAY IT WILL BURN!"***

I said, "How will it burn?"

He said, "Remember what I am telling you, because you will go on television, on the radio and in churches. You must yell with a loud voice. Do not be afraid, because I will be with you."

I said, "How will I be able to go? Who knows me here in America? I don't know anybody here."

He said, "Don't worry yourself. I will go before you. I

will do a lot of healing in the American churches, and I will open the doors for you. But do not say anything else besides what I tell you. This country will burn!"

I said, "What will you do with the Church?"

He said, "I want to save the Church, but the churches have forsaken me."

I said, "How did they forsake you?"

He said, "The people praise themselves. The honor that the people are supposed to give Jesus Christ, they take upon themselves. In the churches there are divorces. There is adultery in the churches. There are homosexuals in the churches. There is abortion in the churches; and all other sins that are possible. Because of the sin, I have left some of the churches. You must yell in a loud voice that they must put an end to their sinning. **They must turn toward the Lord.** The Lord never gets tired of forgiving. They must draw close to the Lord, and live a clean live. If they have sinned until now, they must put an end to it, and start a new life as the Bible tells them to live."

I said, "How will America burn? America is the most powerful country in this world. Why did you bring us here to burn? Why didn't you at least let us die where ALL the Dudumans have died?"

He said, "Remember this, Dumitru. The Russian spies have discovered where the nuclear warehouses are in America. When the Americans will think that it is peace and safety - from the middle of the country, some of the people will start fighting against the government. The government will be busy with internal problems. Then from the ocean, from Cuba, Nicaragua, Mexico,..." (He told me two other countries, but I didn't remember what they were.) "...they will bomb the nuclear warehouses. When they explode, America will burn!"

"What will you do with the Church of the Lord? How

will you save the ones that will turn toward you?" I asked.

He said, "Tell them this: **how I saved the three young ones from the furnace of fire, and how I saved Daniel in the lions den, is the same way I will save them.**"

The angel of the Lord also told me, "I have blessed this country because of the Jewish people who are in this country. I have seven million Jews in this country, but they do not want to recognize the Lord. They didn't want to thank God for the blessings they received in this country."

"Israel doesn't want to recognize Jesus Christ. They put their faith in the Jewish people in America. But, when America burns, the Lord will raise China, Japan and other nations to go against the Russians. They will beat the Russians and push them all the way to the gates of Paris. Over there they will make a treaty, and appoint the Russians as their leaders. They will then unite against Israel."

"When Israel realizes she does not have the strength of America behind her, she will be frightened. That's when she will turn to the Messiah for deliverance. That's when the Messiah will come. Then, the church will meet Jesus in the air, and He will bring them back with Him to the Mount of Olives. At that time the battle of Armageddon will be fought."

When I heard all of this I said, "If you are truly the angel of the Lord, and everything you have told me is true, then all you have said must be written in the Bible."

He said, "Tell everyone to read from **Jeremiah 51:8-15, Revelation chapter 18**, and **Zechariah chapter 14**, where Christ fights against those who possess the earth. After His victory," the angel said, "there will be one flock and one Shepherd. There will be no need for light. The Lamb of God will be the Light. There will be no sickness, no tears, and no deaths. There will only be eternal joy and God will be the ruler. There will be only one language. Only one

162

song. And no need for a translator!"

"And, Dumitru," he continued, "a word of warning. If you keep anything from the American people that you are told, I will punish you severely."

"How will I know that this is for real - that it will really happen?" I asked.

"As a sign that I have spoken to you, tomorrow before you wake I will send someone to bring you a bed, and at noon I will send you a car and a bucket of honey. After which, I will send someone to pay your rent." *(see chapter 10)*

Then the angel left.

Why did God name America MYSTERY BABYLON?

1984

"Tell them, because all the nations of the world immigrated to America with their own gods and were not stopped. Encouraged by the freedom here, the wickedness began to increase. Later on, even though America was established as a Christian nation, the American people began to follow the strange gods that the immigrants had brought in, and also turned their backs on the God who had built and prospered this country."

ANGEL ON A RED HORSE

February 19, 1989

I was asleep this afternoon, when I was awakened by

the whinny of a horse, and the crack of a whip! As I opened my eyes, I saw a man on a red horse. "Get up, Dumitru!" the man said. As I stood up, I was immediately knocked down by his power. "Get up!" he repeated. I stood up, but I was knocked down again. I got up, and was knocked down a third time. I asked him why he did that to me. "To show you my power," he said.

The man was ready for war. He wore a helmet, had guns and knives all around his waist, a machine gun hung around his neck, and he had a sword in one hand. He said, "I am an angel, and have been sent down by Gabriel. Why is your heart so sad because many people don't accept the message? People are happy because there is peace here, but in a short while it will change into war!! I am sent to take peace off the earth." **(Revelation 6:3-4)**

The angel went on, "In some places, wars will start. People will raise their swords against one another." He continued, "Don't be worried, but be happy! Why are you worried about the money? The cries, prayers, and fasting of the ones in your country (Romania) have reached God. Don't be Worried! Gold, silver and wealth belong to God. He will not let you down. You see, some people," said the angel, "don't want to believe the truth or the things that will happen. ONLY THE ONES WHO'S NAMES ARE WRITTEN IN THE BOOK OF LIFE WILL LISTEN AND REPENT! Fight hard, because the fight will be harder as you continue. It will be harder than it has ever been until now," he said. **"The days are numbered, and what I have told you <u>will</u> happen."**

With a noise like thunder and a flash of bright light, he knocked me down a final time and disappeared.

THE VISION OF THE MOUNTAIN

June 1989

While I was in Wisconsin at a pastor's home, during a time of fasting and prayer, a sadness flooded me. I went into my room and began to pray in tongues. Suddenly, a huge mountain appeared before me. Half of the mountain flourished with green trees, and the other half was barren and desolate. Then I heard a big explosion, and a powerful voice said, "California is burning! California is burning! Climb to the top of the mountain! There you will be safe!"

I was desperate because my family was not with me, but in California. So I began to call for them. I saw California engulfed in flames. I began to climb the mountain, and when I looked back, I saw my wife dragging my three grandsons by the hand. "Get up here faster so you won't burn!" I shouted. Then I saw my daughter helping her husband along, because he was afraid of falling. "Tell them not to look back," the voice called. I yelled his instructions to them, and told them to hurry so they wouldn't catch on fire.

Finally, all of us were on the top of the mountain. "Look down." the voice said. Looking down, I saw fire bursting out of the ground, while trees and houses disintegrated before my eyes. People were screaming in agony and pain. I saw some of them trying to climb up the mountain, but most of them weren't able to. Then, two men dressed in white appeared. One of them said in a loud voice, "Do you see how California is burning? This is how it will happen."

Trembling with fear, I reappeared in the pastor's backyard. Flames were erupting out of the ground, so I began to scream, "Get out of the house and climb up the

165

mountain so you won't burn! America is burning!" Running out of the house, they screamed, "Save us, Jesus!" Confused, I saw the two men dressed in white appearing again. One of them said, "See what I have shown you? This is how it will happen. The mountain that you see before you is Jesus Christ. Those who live a holy life will be saved. When the attack comes and the country burns, only those who's names are written in the Book of Life will be saved. Remember to tell everybody what I have shown you."

When the vision ended, I told the pastor what happened and called my family right away. "Is there any fire? Has anything happened?" I asked. Hearing that nothing happened, I was overjoyed.

By standing on the mountain, we will be saved.

REVOLUTION IN ROMANIA

June 1989

As we continued to pray, asking the Lord when these things would happen to America, I had a message from God telling me, "Don't be afraid. First, there will be a revolution in Romania, and then the troubles will come upon America. However, things will get better in Romania before anything happens to this country."

THE STAR

December 5, 1989

I had just returned home from Wisconsin. Every time I prayed, a very big star would appear in front of me. This happened about sixteen times in a period of a few days. Every time the star would appear, it would make a **great noise** and I would always tremble. For a few seconds it would just stand up high and then, at **great speed** it would **fall** to the ground! I prayed together with my family for an answer.

After the 16th time, the answer came. I heard a voice say, "Do you see this star? It represents America. **This is how fast the fall of America will be!** As fast as that star fell!"

Then the voice said, "I love the Christians in this country because of all the good deeds they have done, and for the help they have given those in need. I blessed this country so other people would be fed from it."

The voice also said, "There will be a time of preparation for the people. The ones who need to repent should do it now, before it is too late. The time without trouble will last until the total number of the chosen is fulfilled." (Obadiah 1:4)

My prayer is that God will have mercy on this nation.

RETURN TO ROMANIA

January 1990

I had resigned myself to the fact that I would never be able to return to Romania.

While I was sitting on my bed in a motel room in Michigan, a pillar of light appeared before me. The light was very powerful. Inside the light I saw a face. A voice said, "You will be going to Romania, but do not be afraid, for I will be with you and nothing will happen to you. You will return to your home in peace. "

Then he told me, "Do not cease to tell my people to repent, for a short time will pass, then I will start judging the ones who now dishonor and disobey me." Then the light disappeared.

With joy and courage in my heart I said, "If God is with me who can be against me?"

BIRD ON THE PLANE

April 1990

While coming back from Romania I was given this vision: As I was sitting in the seat, a white bird with a golden and shiney beak appeared. In it's beak it had a letter which it opened with it's feet and a voice said, "Read."

The letter said, "I was with you in Romania and I am with you now while you return. Because you were not partial and you gave to everybody....because you obeyed and did as I told you to do...my blessings will be over you even more than they have been. Do everything that I put in your heart to do, and I the Lord will help you. I will open the doors which were not opened until now, and I will bless you so you can work for Me. I am with you." Then the bird closed the letter, and waving good bye with it's wing, disappeared.

THE CAMP OF GOD

June 6,1990

On the night of June 6th I couldn't sleep, but with troubling thoughts, the time passed fast enough. When I looked at the clock it was already midnight. Getting on my knees I spent quite a while praying, and afterwards I went to bed. The dream that I had that night made me shake all over. It terrified me.

In front of me appeared a man with a handsome face, but he was very big. Standing, he could reach the heavens with his head, but his feet were not on anything solid. There was thunder coming out of his mouth. He took the stars, the moon, and the sun and put them in a tent. Then I saw no more land or people, but only the skies which were like water. I became frightened and asked, "What is happening here? Where are all the people?"

He then showed me a very big tent. Through the crack of the door I saw a very bright light. It was so powerful that I couldn't look at it straight. Through the lightning I heard a voice that said, "Behold, this is the camp of God, in which sit the chosen ones."

When I looked through the light of the tent I saw Christ. Than I heard a voice say, "These are all my redeemed which are on the earth who have a clean life and who are washed in my blood."

After that I heard a loud clap of thunder. Then I woke up. I went and told my family and now I wanted to share it with you.

Revelation 21:3, *"And I heard a loud voice from heaven saying, "Behold, the tabernacle of God is with men, and He will dwell with them, and they shall be His people, and God Himself will be with them and be* *their God."*

WHEN WILL IT HAPPEN?

1991

So many people were asking, "When will it happen? When Will America burn?" I prayed and asked God, "What will I tell people when they ask me when it will happen?" That night an angel came and touched me on the hand and said, "Dumitru, wake up! Sit up! Get your Bible and read **Hosea 4:6-9** and **Hosea 6:1-3**."

"Tell the people of America that one day with the Lord is as a thousand years, and a thousand years as one day. If they will repent and turn back to God, they will make it through the second day to the third day. If they don't, they will not make it."

II Peter 3:8, *"But, beloved, be not ignorant of this one thing, that one day is with the Lord as a thousand years, and a thousand years as one day."*

"FEAR ME & DRAW CLOSER"

March 1991

Romans 1:18, *"For the wrath of God is revealed from heaven against all ungodliness and unrighteousness of men, who suppress the truth in unrighteousness."*

The angel of God visited me two times in one week. The first visit was on the ninth of March at about 5:00 p.m. Suddenly I felt a great weakness pass over me. I went and laid in bed thinking that I was exhausted and needed to rest. At once a being appeared before me. He was dressed in white, and his face shone so brightly that you could not see his features. He shook me and said, "Wake up for I must tell you something." When I opened my eyes I saw the angel of God had a piece of paper that was written in Hebrew. He said, "Read". When I began to look at the letters they turned into Romanian. The scroll read: "Do not cease to tell people to fear me and draw closer to me..." That was all I had a chance to read because one of my grandsons jumped on my legs, and everything disappeared.

I was very saddened, so I began to pray earnestly that the angel would return with the rest of the message. I spent the next few days mostly in prayer. Then, a man dressed in white appeared. He looked very strange to me because he looked like an ordinary man. I thought of asking him who he was, but before I got a chance to say a word, he began to talk to me. "Everything I have shown you, and told you are things that happened, are happening, and will happen. Do not forget to tell everyone to worship God with all their heart." He continued with encouragement, and some direction for me personally, and for my family. When he finished, I asked, "Who are you?"

"I am the one who is, and was, and will always be with you," he said. When he finished this sentence he was suddenly surrounded by a powerful burst of light, and he disappeared.

A FLICKER OF LIGHT

May 1991

In my dream, the sun and the moon appeared in the

heavens in a powerful intensity I had never seen before. Suddenly two men came out of the light; one out of the sun, and one out of the moon. The one in the sun began to speak. "I am the Son of Righteousness, and I will soon come to judge the world! Get up and work NOW while it is still day, for night is soon coming when you no longer shall be able to work. I want to strengthen you, for I still have work for you to do. Look to your left."

When I looked to my left, I saw a black cloud furiously approaching, with lightning and thunder booming out of it! It covered the horizon, and soon covered the sun and moon. A heavy smell filled the place where I stood, making it very difficult to breathe. "What can this horrible stench be?," I asked.

"This is how nuclear fallout smells," He replied.

Then suddenly, in the darkness of the cloud, far away from where I stood, there was a little flicker of light. The Voice in the sun said, "Walk toward the light."

As I began to follow the flicker of light, all of my family was suddenly with me. We kept walking on a very narrow path, and after a very long and exhausting trip we arrived at the bank of a big body of water. Again the Voice spoke, "You must get across the water!" I became troubled, because there was no way we could cross. Then something like a ski lift appeared before us. The voice again spoke, "Get on." Before we even had time to think, we arrived on the other side of the body of water. Then the voice said to me, "Do not be quiet. Tell the people that time is very short, and the trouble WILL come onto the earth. I will still allow a time for the souls of those that I want to save. Tell the people that I am a jealous God, and I want them all for me. Tell them to pray more and worship me with all their hearts in holiness, and cleanliness."

Then I awoke......

HEAVENLY VISITORS

August 1991

It was hard for me to fall asleep last night. I prayed a lot. When I finally fell asleep, I had a dream.

I was in a valley with mountains around it. Someone yelled at me, "Run and hide! Rain is coming!"

I thought, "I'm not afraid of the rain." I looked around and could not see anyone. Then I heard peals of thunder! A powerful bolt of lightening passed right by me! Out of it came two beings!

They asked if I was afraid. I said, "Yes." They asked if I knew who they were. I said "No."

They said, "We are heavenly beings." Their clothes were white as snow. They had eyes that were penetrating. There was a light in them so bright I could hardly look at them. Their hair was white as wool, and it was long, going down their backs. One of them had a book and the other had an ink well attached to his belt, and a large pen in his hand. There was an eraser on one end.

The one with the pen said, "I was sent to complete the book of the Gentiles. Do you want to see your names?" I looked and saw that all the names of my family were written there, and they were circled. I asked why the were circled. He said, "The devil doesn't like what you do and fights powerfully against all you do. I have circled your names so I can give you extra protection."

He opened the back of the book and counted out 4 remaining blank pages at the end. "When these are filled," he said, "the book of the Gentiles will be complete. Then I will return to my people. Some of the names that are listed here will be erased. I will erase the names of those who have mocked God and tested the Spirit of Grace. I will

173

replace them with other names."

I started to ask what the 4 pages meant, but before I could ask the meaning, he thrust the pen into the ink well, as though slipping a sword into a scabbard. As he did, there was such tremendous thunder and lightening that I fell down. Then I woke up.

CLOUDS IN THE SKIES

1991

After I prayed I went to sleep. While I was sleeping I dreamed someone was telling me, "Rain is coming!"

I looked around but saw no one. But suddenly there was thunder and lightening, and a red cloud appeared. In it's midst were the hammer and sickle of Communism. On the other side was another cloud, but with no unusual colors. Suddenly, an intensely bright star appeared out of the cloud. Then the red cloud began to surround the cloud with the star, and tried to capture it. Immediately, a white cloud appeared, bursting forth with great thunder and lightening. When it appeared, the red cloud was dismembered. Then two men appeared out of the white cloud. One had a face like the sun. It was so bright I could not look at it. The other had a humble face, and had a book in his hand. He opened the book, and said, "Look." He began to count the blank pages of the book. There were only three and a quarter empty pages! Then he said. "It won't be long. Be prepared. When these pages are filled, The Grace will leave the gentiles. Draw closer to me now, more than ever - and be holy, because hard times are coming." Then the man with the book said ,"Look to the right." When I looked to the right, I saw a beautiful garden filled with all kinds of flowers. But I had never seen ANY of these kinds before.

Then I woke up.

AMERICA, THE FALLING STAR

January 23, 1992

It was late, on January 23rd. After prayer I went to sleep. In my dream, I heard a loud noise. I began to look around me. When I looked up, I saw a big star in the sky but, it's tips were bent. Suddenly, I heard the sound of hoofbeats, which were getting closer and closer. When I looked where the noise was coming form, I saw four horses pulling an old fashioned chariot. In the chariot were four men. They were armed with heavy artillery and they began to shoot at the star. The star began to burn. Then it fell from the sky. I woke up and told Mike the dream. He asked me what it meant. When I told him I didn't know, he told me to pray, and if it was of God, He would let me dream it again.

I prayed, and again tried to fall asleep. I was nodding off, when again I heard the noise and saw the star with it's bent tips. Again I heard the hoofbeats. But this time when I looked up, there were six horses and six men in the chariot. All of them had masks on and they were armed. Again they began to shoot at the star. The star began to burn again and fell. Frightened, I woke up. Being troubled, I prayed again and asked God for an explanation. I could not fall asleep for a few hours, but when I did, the same dream came again. This time the noise was even greater. Again the star appeared, with the same crooked tips. Again I heard the horses. This time though, there weren't four or six horses. There were EIGHT horses; and EIGHT men were in the chariot. Again they fired upon the star, and it fell. This time, when it hit the ground, it blew up. In the same place where the star used to be, appeared a man dressed in white. He said, "The star represents America. The reason the tips are crooked, is because America has fallen away from the Truth, and the Way of God. The eight horses, and the men in the chariot, represent eight kings that will rise up against America and will overcome her." Then the dream ended.

That same morning, during my prayer time, I saw a red flag with light blue and white in the left corner. It was bleeding. May God keep us awake, and ready.

MAN HOLDING THE MOON

June 3, 1992

I dreamed I was on the shore of a river. When I looked into the water I saw that it was very dirty. I wanted to catch fish, but I couldn't because the waters were so muddy. I asked myself, "How can I catch fish from this river? There is no clean water anywhere to clean up afterwards."

When I looked further up the river, I saw a large patch of clean water coming. When it came by me, I checked the clean water with my hand to see if it was cold. When I felt the water, a powerful ray of light came down surrounding me. The light enabled me to see many fish. I was surprised to see how many fish were there.

When I looked up, I saw the light was coming from the moon. When I looked closer, I saw a man in the moon. His face was so shinny I could not look long. I looked back into the water. A voice told me, "Start fishing now, because the time is very short. Soon there will be no more opportunity to fish." The voice sounded so close it frightened me. The man looked so far away, but the voice was close. I looked up. Then I heard the voice again. The man said, "The ray of light that you see is my voice."

Then he said, "Look how many fish are before you." When I looked down I saw many more fish than before. The man said the second time, "Catch them now. Fish now. Fish while you can. For in a short time the fishing shall be over." When I looked back toward the moon, it had changed into a red arch, like a rainbow. The man was holding it in his hand by a corner. He said to me, "See this moon? Soon it's light will go out." I asked, "Where am I?" Then I woke up.

Revelation 8:12, *"Then the fourth angel sounded: and a third of the sun was struck, and a third of the moon, and a third of the stars, so that a third of them were darkened; and a third of the day did not shine, and likewise the night."*

Isaiah 13:10, *"For the stars of heaven and their constellations will not give their light; The sun will be darkened in its going forth, and the moon will not cause its light to shine."*

Isaiah 24:21, *"It shall come to pass in that day that the Lord will punish on high the host of exalted ones, and on the earth the kings of the earth."*

THE DUDUMAN FAMILY IN 1971 - I AM THE SECOND FROM THE RIGHT

Chapter Thirteen

PHOTOGRAPHS

BROTHER DUMITRU DUDUMAN
- 1991 -

179

**POSING IN ROMANIA WITH MY GRANDSONS,
MY DOG LABUS, AND CAT COSTIN**

MY FAMILY IN FULLERTON, CALIFORNIA - 1986...

...AND IN 1990

181

- "MOST PRECIOUS GIFT" -

On our first trip back to Romania in 1990, my daughter, Virginia, and I were able to take 300 large print study Bibles with us. This is one of them. Praise God!

**I WAS EXCITED TO BE ABLE TO GIVE THIS STUDY BIBLE TO MY
FRIEND, A BAPTIST PASTOR IN SUCEAVA, ROMANIA**

**GIVING BIBLES TO AN OLD FRIEND OF MINE - ONE FOR HIM AND
ONE FOR A PASTOR IN HIS VILLAGE**

IN 1991, I WAS ABLE TO DISTRIBUTE 20,000 OF THESE ROMANIAN
NEW TESTAMENTS THROUGH "HAND OF HELP"

PART OF THE ROMANIAN NEW TESTAMENTS WENT TO ROMANIAN
SPEAKING RUSSIANS IN MOLDAVIA, RUSSIA

**GREETINGS FROM THE ROMANIAN/RUSSIAN MOLDAVIA BORDER
WHERE I WAS ABLE TO FREELY CROSS ON JUNE 16, 1991**

185

WHENEVER WE BRING EMIGRATING ROMANIANS INTO THE U.S., WE SHARE A CELEBRATION FEAST WITH THEM IN OUR HOME

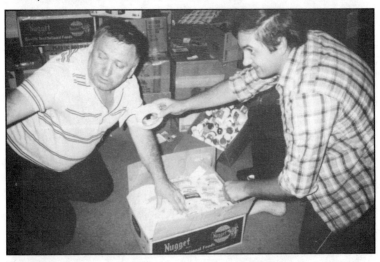

A FRIEND HELPING ME PACK A BOX OF FOOD FOR SHIPMENT TO A NEEDY FAMILY IN ROMANIA - UNTIL 1992, WE WOULD SHIP THIS WAY

BOXES OF FOOD, CLOTHING, AND MEDICAL SUPPLIES PREPARED FOR SHIPPING BY *CONTAINER* **- TODAY'S CHEAPER METHOD**

ON THE PLANE TO ROMANIA WITH VIRGINIA AND MIKE, JR. TO PERSONALLY SEE THAT THE CONTAINERS ARE DISTRIBUTED

187

**GROUNDBREAKING FOR THE NEW "HAND OF HELP"
ORPHANAGE - JUNE 1991**

ASSISTING IN BAPTISM IN ROMANIA

**IN EARNEST PRAYER, BEFORE BAPTISM IN THE BLACK SEA
- CONSTANSA, ROMANIA - 1991**

189

PASSING OUT TOYS AT THE STATE ORPHANAGE IN BOTOSANI FOR 3-5 YEAR-OLDS (1991)

PASSING OUT NEW TESTAMENTS AND TRACTS AT A CRUSADE

**ROMANIAN ORTHODOX CHURCH - BUILT BY ORDER OF
"STEPHEN THE GREAT" IN THE 15TH CENTURY - SUCEAVA**

**NEW CHURCH IN TALPA - BUILT WITH DONATIONS
GIVEN THROUGH "HAND OF HELP"**

191

**SHARING MY TESTIMONY AT AN "OPEN DOORS" CONFERENCE
SACRAMENTO, CALIFORNIA - OCTOBER 4, 1986**

**BUDD AND JOANNE TUBBS HAVE BEEN WITH US FROM THE
BEGINNING OF OUR "HAND OF HELP" MINISTRY - (PHOTO - 1990)**

BAPTIZING MY GRANDSON, MIKE - CALIFORNIA - JUNE 1988

ON THE ROAD IN AMERICA, SHARING MY TESTIMONY - WITH MIKE (MY GRANDSON AND INTERPRETER) AND SISTER SHERRY - SEPTEMBER 1988

THE JOY OF THE LORD SHINES, EVEN IN THE FACES OF THE POOREST VILLAGERS SUCH AS THIS MAN

**THIS IS TYPICAL OF THE POOREST VILLAGES IN ROMANIA
- THESE ARE <u>HOMES!</u> -**

**THE POOR WIDOWS ARE ALWAYS HAPPY TO RECEIVE FOOD FROM
THE "HAND OF HELP" MISSION (PHOTO - JUNE 1991)**

195

VISITING MY BROTHER, COSTACHE FOR THE FIRST TIME IN SIX YEARS - *SEE CHAPTER 1, PAGE 11 -*

WHILE VISITING ROMANIA, I OFTEN STOP ALONG THE ROAD AND GIVE TO THE POOR AS GOD DIRECTS ME - IT IS A REAL JOY

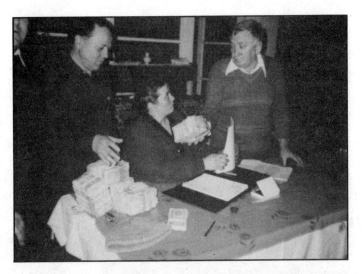

MONEY TO HELP BUILD A CHURCH - MANY LEI (ROMANIAN CURRENCY), BUT FEW US$

THE CHOIR FROM BOTOSANI CHURCH #1 - THEY SOMETIMES TRAVEL WITH ME WHEN I EVANGELIZE IN ROMANIA (PHOTO - 1991)

CONTAINER OF FOOD, CLOTHING, AND MEDICAL SUPPLIES BOUND FOR ROMANIA - <u>CAN YOU HELP?</u> (see chapter 11, page 158)